"What a historical gem! In a manner rendered moot by today's texts and Tweets, Adelaide Kibbe's carefully written and preserved letters open our eyes to another time and place in history. And yet, for all who have traveled between cultural worlds, she tells a modern story too, for it is ultimately a human story.

While the details are different – taking long sea passages across the ocean rather than long haul jets – we understand the excitement of new things another culture offers – to see and taste and do. We smile as we identify how these once intriguing differences have become so commonplace we barely notice them. We understand the loneliness separation from friends and relatives brings. But Dr. Kibbe's story tells us so much more.

In a day when female doctors were rare and their medical skills suspect, she had such confidence in her calling and personal identity she never wasted breath trying to prove gender equality. She let her life and work speak for itself.

And finally, it is the story of what one life can accomplish and achieve when lived for something more than self. In a 'me-first' world, she shows us how in giving her life to serve those from another land, culture, and economic status she also found it. A great read."

Ruth E Van Reken,
Author, *Third Culture Kids: Growing Up Among Worlds*, and *Letters Never Sent*
www.crossculturalkid.org

Passage to Persia:

Writings of an American doctor during her life in Iran, 1929-1957

by
Margaret A Frame

Passage to Persia by Margaret A Frame

First Edition 2014

First Published in the United Kingdom by Summertime Publishing
© Copyright Margaret A Frame

ISBN 978-1-909193-57-4

This book is dedicated to all the women missionary doctors who spent their lives giving of their talents and love so that the sick in body and mind could be healed,

and

To Adelaide Kibbe's descendants and extended family, that they may be inspired by her journey.

Acknowledgements

While writing this book, I asked many friends and family to read and comment on sections as the work progressed. I am grateful for all their helpful comments, editing, and proofreading. My friend and former schoolmate Dr. Michael Zirinsky graciously wrote the Foreword for this book. He has written numerous articles and contributed to books about Iran and its historical relations with the west, as well as the Presbyterian Missionaries influence in Iran during the early twentieth century. Special thanks to Mary Evans Swope for her hours correcting my typos, punctuation and suggestions for where I needed to include footnotes. My thanks to the Presbyterian Historical Society Staff and Reference Librarians at Berkeley Public Library for helping me locate material, and not least of all, my editors and designer at Summertime Publishing, Jo Parfitt, Jane Dean and Owen Jones (www.owenjonesdesign.com).

Contents

Foreword

Dr. Adelaide Kibbe Frame Hoffman served as a Presbyterian missionary physician in northern Iran during four decades, arriving in the 1920s and retiring only in the later 1950s. During these years she observed Iran's transformation from an isolated traditional society into a modernizing nation-state intimately involved in international affairs. Dr. Kibbe experienced Iran's enormous twentieth century development, and her writings offer an excellent window from which we can peer into the Persian past as well as at America's first, altruistic and well-received encounter with Iran.

Americans first came to Iran in the late 1820s as part of a worldwide religious awakening. A first American mission station was established near the Turkish and Russian borders at Urmia in the early 1830s, and after responsibility for this enterprise was transferred to the Presbyterian Board of Foreign Missions in New York City in the 1880s, other stations were established throughout northern Iran.

In practice, missionary activity – preaching Christianity, teaching in western-style schools and providing modern medical care – focused on secular work: education and medicine. Few Iranians wanted to become American Protestants, but many hungered for the European languages, practical curriculum and medicine on offer. American schools and hospitals thus became an important vector of globalizing change for Iran, until the spread of Iranian-financed schools and hospitals made the missionaries secular work redundant.

The US had no diplomatic representation in Iran for the first half-century of the mission's existence. Until late 1941 when it entered the Second World War as an ally of Britain and Russia against Germany, America opposed all imperial designs on Iran. Consequently, Iranians looked favorably on Americans, especially as Tehran sought a "third power" to bring into the balance against Britain and Russia – both of whom made war on Iran in the nineteenth century and who in 1907 partitioned the country into "spheres of influence."

In early 1911, during the closing phase of the Iranian Constitutional Revolution (1906-11), the new Iranian parliamentary government hired American financier Morgan Shuster to head its treasury. Shuster – whose office was staffed by Iranians trained in American mission schools – was soon fired by the Russians and British, who consolidated their control over the country by the end of the year in a process Shuster called "the strangling of Persia."

Since Iran effectively was occupied by Russian and British forces after 1911, it became a battlefield of the First World War, despite declaring its neutrality. As a result of battles, famine and epidemic disease exacerbated by the conflict, Iran fell into anarchy, loosing perhaps one quarter of its population and seeing foreign troops manoeuver at will on its soil. Britain refused to allow Iran a seat at the 1919 Paris Peace Conference and sought instead to bring "order" to what its representative at Tehran, Major-General Sir Percy Z. Cox called, *"one of the outstanding ulcers of chaos in the civilized world,"* by inducing Iran to accept the 1919 Anglo-Persian Agreement (FO248/1211).

Iranian hope for American assistance continued, however. Encouraged by the US, Tehran refused to ratify the 1919 Agreement. Instead, it decided again to employ a private American mission, this time headed by Arthur Millspaugh (formerly the State Department's Petroleum Advisor), to regulate the Iranian treasury. Millspaugh's mission (1922-27), which also employed many alumni of the mission schools, created an efficient revenue system, making possible many subsequent reforms, financed by Iran without foreign loans or grants.

Thus during the decades Dr. Kibbe served in Iran the country underwent tremendous change. Some efforts, such as the insistence by Tehran that foreigners refer to the country by its own name, Iran, rather than by foreign terms such as "Persia," and that men wear western-style hats with brims instead of traditional Iranian headgear, clearly were superficial. Others had deep and revolutionary impact on the country, such as transport improvements which made road travel within Iran secure and cheap and which cut the time needed to journey from New York to Tehran, for example, to hours instead of weeks or even months.

Before progress was interrupted by the Second World War, Iran shed the hated "capitulations" (unequal treaties which gave foreigners extraterritorial rights and consular jurisdiction), established western-style law codes and courts, began building schools for boys and girls in expectation of eventual universal education, established a university at Tehran, and required women to wear western-style clothing in public, forbidding traditional *chaddors* to maintain public modesty. Traditional buildings were pulled down in favor of western-style structures, and private properties were bisected again and again as straight roads replaced traditional paths. The greatest achievement, at least in monetary cost, was the building of a Trans-Iranian Railway which, rather than tying Iran into an international rail network including Turkey, Russia and India, was located to facilitate sending troops to restive, tribal-controlled areas. In retrospect, it seems that many of the changes were designed to raise central government authority by breaking the power of local notables, foreigners and even the *ulema* (Islamic clergy) who formerly had staffed law courts and schools.

These transformations took place during the Pahlavi era (1921-1979), named after Reza Pahlavi, who seized power in a February 1921 coup and made himself king by 1926. Reza Shah was succeeded by his son Mohammed Reza Shah Pahlavi, who reigned from 1941 to 1979.

Reza Shah's emergence, reign and legacy is controversial. Many Iranians believe he was made king by a British plot. Although he did have tangible support from British agents for his February 1921 coup d'état, in my view it seems clear that he was able to gain power primarily by riding a national wave of disgust against the chaos and impotence of the last years of the Qajar dynasty. He was a soldier, an imposing, intelligent, patriotic six-footer who rose from the ranks by talent and performance to command the Cossacks, the once Russian-officered force, which seized Tehran in late February 1921. Because of his clear vision, political acumen and brutal tactics, he was able to gain support from most segments of Iranian opinion, from bureaucrats, merchants, landowners and *ulema*, as well as from foreigners. Those who opposed him, he crushed. Britain supported him reluctantly, after despairing of any other solution to the chaos it feared on its Indian and Arab frontiers, especially as it worried about renewed aggression from Communist Russia. Ironically, the Soviets also supported Reza's rise, seeing his regime as a buffer against "imperialist expansionism."

Despite the enormous efforts Reza Shah made to modernize Iran and build up its military forces, he was unmade by the west. Following

Hitler's attack on the Soviets in June 1941 Britain and Russia again allied against Germany and invaded Iran in August 1941 as part of their grand strategy to defeat the Nazis, by securing Iranian oil for the British war effort and opening a supply route for American Lend-Lease supplies to Russia. In September Reza abdicated in favor of his son Mohammed Reza. The new young Shah – only 21 when he succeeded his father – was a weak actor in Iranian politics until August 1953, when an Anglo-American inspired "anti-Communist" coup enabled him to grasp all the levers of power in the country and to resume his father's path as a military dictator imposing western-style change on the country. As we all know, the Shah's regime preceded the 1978-79 revolution, which ushered in the Islamic Republic.

Reza Shah admired Mustafa Kemal's leadership of Turkey[1]. The Ottoman Empire, Iran's western rival for over 400 years, also had disintegrated following defeat in the First World War. Under Kemal's leadership Turkey emerged from the Ottoman ruins as a strong modern nation-state, capable of defending its borders and earning the respect of western powers. Consequently many observers believe that Reza and his advisors sought to copy Kemal: continuing outward, western-style constitutional forms under control of military dictatorship, building modern roads and western-style buildings, encouraging universal access to modern education and medical care, decreasing the role of Islam in secular society and so forth.

The differences between Iran and Turkey are enormous. The process of responding to western pressure by "modernization" had begun in the Ottoman Empire at the end of the eighteenth century,

---

1   Mustafa Kemal was also called Atatürk, father of Turkey

but in Iran it began only a century later. Kemal was a product of the century old modern Turkish military academies, highly educated by the standards of his day to be part of the Empire's governing elite. He was a successful general both during the Great War and afterwards, in the war of independence against Greece. Reza, by comparison, was an unschooled product of the Iranian periphery, molded by Cossack whips rather than by teachers, untested in foreign war. So Reza's efforts to do as Kemal had done were quite different in both method and effect.

The difference can be seen most starkly in foreign policy. Both Turkey and Iran had longstanding enmities with both Russia and Britain, and consequently encouraged German efforts to build close relations. Turkey allied with Germany during World War I; Iran's sympathies then also were with the Central Powers, rather than with the occupying British and Russians. When World War II broke out in September 1939, both Turkey and Iran declared neutrality. Atatürk's heirs were able to maintain Turkish independence, largely by adroit diplomacy. Reza Shah, on the other hand, refused to accept British warnings that the Germans were planning to turn Iran into an Axis ally, even after the Nazi attack on Soviet Russia. Britain believed its control of Iranian oil – which it feared might fall to Germany if Reza did not expel all Germans – was essential to its war effort. Reza wished to regain Iranian control over this Iranian resource, as did all patriotic Iranians, and disregarded British protests. So Reza Shah and his army were completely surprised by the Anglo-Soviet invasion of August 1941, which led to a renewed Anglo-Russian partition of Iran, very much like the one following the 1907 Anglo-Russian Convention. In effect, Reza Pahlavi was forced to abdicate in favor of his son in September 1941 to preserve his dynasty. Exiled by Britain to South Africa, Reza Shah soon died.

He did not live long enough to see Russia's postwar effort to maintain control in northern Iran by sponsoring "autonomous republics" in Azerbaijan and Kurdistan, rebellions which were suppressed by Tehran as a first battle of the Cold War. Pahlavi Iran's subsequent alliance with Washington thus was mediated by both Iran's long altruistic experience with American missionaries, including Dr. Kibbe, and US government support of Iranian independence and territorial integrity in 1911, 1919, 1922-27 and again in 1946.

Between 1946 and 1953 Iranian politics were roiled by many factors, including the new Shah's efforts to dominate Iran, nationalist efforts to assert Iranian control over the British government-owned Anglo-Iranian Oil Company, Soviet encouragement of the Tudeh Party and continuing efforts by landowners, bazaar merchants and *ulema* to assert control of the government. The struggle led to the formation of the National Front, a coalition dominated by Dr. Mohammed Mossadegh, a European educated Qajar, who had supported Reza Pahlavi as Prime Minister but spoke against his becoming Shah. After surviving internal exile during 1926-41, Mossadegh resumed political activity, making oil nationalization his signature issue. In 1951 the Shah appointed him Prime Minister, and the Majlis promptly nationalized AIOC's Iranian properties. This set off a confrontation with Britain, which immediately began scheming to overthrow Mossadegh.

For two years Washington sought to mediate between London and Tehran. Both governments regarded America as a friend; both refused compromise. In the context of the Cold War and the war in Korea, this intransigence forced America to choose between its most important military ally or militarily insignificant Iran. Eventually Washington signed on to a British instigated coup, carried out by the Iranian Army under CIA sponsorship in August 1953. Although putsch planner and CIA historian Donald Wilber told me in a

1987 interview that he and his colleagues wanted Iran to establish a parliamentary government where the king reigned but did not rule, in fact the coup made it possible for the Shah to establish an arbitrary dictatorship.

None of us can see into the future, of course. In Adelaide Kibbe's time in Iran, no one saw the Islamic Republic coming, although today it seems clear that the Pahlavis created the modern Iranian state over which the Ayatollahs now reign. Dr. Kibbe observed the creation of modern Iran, as it transformed from its isolated, weak, disorganized nineteenth century condition into a strong, centralized, military-bureaucratic state. She watched the spread of secure, hard-surfaced modern roads, the building of a railway and the opening of air transport. She observed the spread of telephones and radio, as well as of modern schools in the cities, bringing literacy to more and more children, girls as well as boys, and the development and growth of the modern University of Tehran.

All this modernization was so successful that by the time Dr. Kibbe left Iran the American Presbyterian Mission which she served was winding down its activities, closing its hospitals and turning its churches over to the Iranian Evangelical Church which it had nurtured for over a century. Its schools, except for the one it maintained for its own missionaries' children and other English-speaking children in Tehran, the Community School – which Dr. Kibbe's daughter Margaret Frame and I both attended – had already been transferred to Iranian government control in 1940.

So, as you turn to read the correspondence of Dr. Kibbe and her colleagues, remember that this seemingly obscure life was an essential part of a tremendous worldwide phenomenon. It was of course an aspect of the missionary experience, so vital to America's Protestant tradition. It was also a component of the "dialog of civilizations" which has brought previously separate cultures into increasingly intimate contact with each other. And while politicians and journalists tend to focus on the "clash of civilizations," conflicting patriotic world-views trying to get the upper hand in "the game of nations," the deeper reality may be progress for all.

Michael Zirinsky,
Professor of History Emeritus, Boise State University, USA

Preface

As with many of us upon the death of a parent, I was faced with the task of clearing out and packing up my mother's possessions after her last stroke, hospitalization and death. My mother, Adelaide Kibbe, had spent the first twenty-eight years of her life in Ohio and California, preparing for her life's work as a doctor, the next twenty-eight as a medical missionary in Iran, and the final twenty-eight years learning to be retired and a housewife.

Missionaries are expected to write annual personal reports, contribute to specific station reports – in her case hospital reports – keep in touch with home churches, and write articles for missionary journals. 'Personal Reports' would detail her work and personal feelings as a missionary for the year. 'Station Reports' concerned the work of the Station as a whole, with content contributed by individual missionaries. In contrast, 'Station Letters' were written for publication in Missionary Board and Church newsletters, and various Presbyterian journals. My mother saved copies of most of these reports, articles, and personal letters, as well as her diaries. When packing the belongings I wanted to keep, I boxed up all the paperwork to look at in some future time.

A few years ago I decided 'the future' had come and I needed to look through her writings. I was amazed at the beauty of that writing and the keen observations of life around her during the years of tremendous social and political changes in Iran. When my mother first arrived in Iran in 1929, the country was just beginning its transition to a modern, westernized society. When she retired in 1957 Iran was fully engaged in the 20th century.

This is the story not only of her personal journey as a doctor, missionary, and woman, but also her observations of a country evolving from feudal institutions to a strong country and serious political player in the Middle East. In the later years of the story, I have included my own memories of events and experiences growing up as an American child in another country.

Most of the material is from my mother's first ten years in Iran. After her reassignment from Meshed to Resht, she had more responsibilities both as a doctor, a wife and a mother, leaving her much less time to write. In preparing and editing the material we have chosen to add subheadings to benefit the reader. In the interest of the length of the book, some of the content of personal letters was edited.

Adelaide loved poetry and would cut and keep verses she read in newspapers and magazines. At the end of each chapter I have included one of the verses that were important to her.

A Good Islamic Rule

If you are tempted to reveal,

A tale some one to you has told,

About another, make it pass,

Before you speak, three gates of gold,

Three narrow gates – first, "Is it true?"

Then, "Is it needful?" in your mind.

Give truthful answer, and the next,

Is last and narrowest – "Is it kind?"

And, if to reach your lips at last

It passes through these gateways three,

Then you may tell the tale, nor fear

What the result of speech may be.

Anon 1900,
A Hadees of the Prophet Mohammed, set in English verse

CHAPTER 1

Making the Decision

In September of 1929 a young woman doctor, Adelaide Kibbe, 27 years old, set out to spend her life as a missionary. She had been raised on the stories of her grandparents' experiences as missionaries in China, and had always enjoyed hearing missionaries from Africa and India speak at church. Once she had applied to the Presbyterian Mission Board to be a missionary herself, her dreams were of continuing her grandparents' work in China or going to Africa to see the places she had heard so much about. But the Mission Board had another need for her. The mission work in the Moslem country of Persia desperately needed women doctors. Many women in Persia were not able to get medical care unless they could be treated by a woman. When she was told she would be going to Persia (Iran today), the family didn't even know where the country was. So on the September day when she first saw the place which was to be her home for the next 30 years, it was with a mixture of disappointment that it was not China, and excitement at finally arriving to carry on the family traditions and her decision, made eight years earlier, to be a missionary.

Adelaide was born into a loving, Christian family in Lima, Ohio. Her older brother and sister were eight and nine years older, and proud of their little sister. Her father was fascinated with the new technology of the automobile and in 1905 bought one of the first Fords in town. Adelaide would tell the story of how, terrified, she hid under a blanket on her first ride. All her life she loved to whistle and remembered with great pleasure, when about nine years old, winning the town whistling contest, much to the disgust and chagrin of the boys. When Adelaide was 11, her father moved the family to Berkeley, California. Here she attended High School and then Mills College. She inherited her father's love of the automobile, getting her driver's license in 1917, aged 16, and doing most of the driving on family trips. At Mills College she was active in sports, playing field hockey and participating in track and field events. For the rest of her life she loved to run as a way to unwind after a day at the hospital. The most important part of her life was her involvement in Christian Youth activities, teaching Sunday School, and learning about mission work.

In 1921 when a junior in college, Adelaide Kibbe attended a Young Adult Christian Conference in Asilomar, California. She made the following notations in her diary regarding the decisions she made at the Conference.

Diary entry June 19, 1921:
"Decided 'God willing' to go to foreign field as a lab worker or teacher. Now I have something definite to work for. Spent half an hour on dunes overlooking ocean, alone."

A few days later after the conference she writes:
"I don't need anything to remind me of my big decision to serve Christ in foreign field or anywhere I can – God willing – it is before me always as my hope and may I get strength for it from above."

In August when she returned to school and again tackled lab work she noted:
"Will I ever be able to be a lab worker and get through Chemistry?"

The following year, 1922, she reread her comments and wrote:
"I read above day's entry and am glad I have decided to be a doctor, if I am suited. I hope someone will tell me if I'm not."

Over the next seven years in preparation for following her calling as a missionary doctor, she went to medical school, undertook an internship in San Francisco and a year residency in New York visiting clinics and working in the New York Infirmary for Women and Children as Resident Physician. During her residency in New York she contracted Rheumatic fever, which continued to affect her all her life with reoccurring bouts and damage to her heart.

In 1927, Adelaide sent a formal application to the Presbyterian Board of Foreign Missions to be a missionary. She had been in contact with the Mission Board since first deciding she wanted to be a missionary in 1922, to express her desire to do missionary work as a doctor. Adelaide still had to complete the Internship and Residency portion of her training, but the time had come to make a final decision and start the paperwork to become a missionary.

Part of the application requirements was to write an essay about her life as a Christian and her personal beliefs.

"My life began in a Christian home, a family with missionary interests, in Lima, Ohio, September 1901. Sunday school and church attendance are among my earliest recollections. I went to the kindergarten and grade schools there until we moved to Berkeley, California, in

1912. I have been in Berkeley since then finishing grade school and high school here, and completing the four years' course at Mills College, Oakland, (as a boarder for the four years) in 1922. That same year I entered the University of California Medical School and have now almost completed the required years of medical work and am to take my year of internship at the University of California Hospital in San Francisco beginning in June 1927, and receiving my degree, therefore in May 1928.

As I stated above, I have lived in a Christian family where Christian love and practices has been the guiding principle so that any credit for early training in the Bible, character development along Christ's teachings belongs to my parents, their wisdom and devotion. At about the of age of thirteen Jesus Christ gradually became a living, vital personality to me – His way of life the only way to be followed, so that I could publically accept Him and join the church. I worked actively in the Sunday School until going to college where I was too far distant to attend our church regularly. During the first two years of my college life I feel that on the surface my Christian development was somewhat passive – though I attended church, enjoyed all courses offered in Biblical literature and entered into biblical clubs and discussions with eagerness and interest. I realize now, that unconsciously, however, I was seeking a goal, a purpose for my life, not knowing definitely what it should be, or how to actively express in living the Christian ideals that I held. The answer came to me at a Student Volunteer Conference attended through the influence of my sister and brother-in-law, both Student Volunteers. I understood, then, that for me only by serving Jesus Christ entirely, giving my life, my talents whatever they might be, to His work could

I ever be truly happy and at peace within myself. At that time, too, as I was interested in science, I decided that medicine afforded the greatest opportunity for me to work for the case of Jesus Christ and his Kingdom. But not until the emotional appeal of such a meeting had subsided, and I saw the facts clearly and what such a future entailed, did I sign the Pledge card. Since that time in 1922 with this one purpose in mind I have "pressed on toward the goal", realizing with a growing conviction, tried by periods of weakness and doubt, that through God's guidance I have decided aright.

I cannot truthfully say that personal evangelism, 'soul winning' is easy for me to do, or that I have made it a part of my daily living, though I admit its value and admire those who can so do. Perhaps, therefore, I have not the true 'missionary spirit'. But I do know this – the result of my Christian development – that I desire with my whole being to help bring to the people of the world who have not had opportunity, or who have not taken it, to know and accept Jesus Christ as Master, to understand that His love is for all mankind, to experience the transforming power of His love, and to follow in the 'Jesus way' of life. If this is not sufficient for a missionary spirit then I am presuming too much in making application. It is against my nature to be otherwise, but not against my will if I could do differently.

My motive in seeking missionary appointment is embodied in my Christian development fostered by a family fundamentally interested in promoting missionary endeavor, in bringing the Kingdom of God to earth by whatever means one can. I feel that in Medical work I can most fully live for Christ, implying, of course, that through the unique advantage offered to a doctor, I, too, by Christ's strength in me, can bring a measure of healing, love, and peace into the world. That is my Christian experience and motive in asking for missionary appointment.

I believe that God is creator of all life, a spirit working in the world, through the souls of men, yet endowed with a Personality that of an all-wise, loving father with implied attributes, to whom we can pray for forgiveness of our sins, to whom we give thanks for all our blessings, upon whom we depend for our life on this earth, and in the life to come.

Jesus Christ is the son of God sent to this earth in human form, yet of a divine nature, that in Him we might behold and understand the Perfect Life, and through whom we have received redemption for our sins. By his death and resurrection do we know that for us there will be Eternal Life.

The Holy Spirit is 'the Helper' sent in Christ's name to dwell in the hearts of men who accept Him, that as Jesus promised they may be guided in His way of Life. I believe that the Holy Spirit works through all of God's agencies here on earth, that by them His Kingdom may more speedily and effectively be brought to completion.

Duties to one's fellowmen seem to me to be most comprehensively summed up in Christ's Sermon on the Mount as found in Matthew 5th, 6th, & 7th chapters.

I believe that the Scriptures are the Word of God [and] that the Old Testament is a history of the development of the knowledge of God as exemplified in the Hebrew race – God's chosen people – a background for the coming of Christ. I do not believe that every word in the Bible can be taken literally but that careful judgment and thought, as directed by God in the reading of it, is necessary to understand and interpret the meaning.

The redemptive work of Christianity is found in Christ's vicarious suffering for our sins, that through Him we may receive forgiveness, not wholly to save us from the consequences of our sins from which we cannot expect to be entirely free, but to save us from the weakness of our wills, the power of sin in our lives, the yielding to temptations and the lack of faith in God.

I believe the church to be an outward expression of our religion – a necessary part of any religious life, to receive and to give the inspiration of common worship and praise of God. I believe that the church should have a definite part in any community where situated, the church members and participants should enter into the community spirit and activities, that through them the Kingdom of God may be more effectively spread.

I believe in religious tolerance and sympathy with people of different creeds, and feel that Christ's Kingdom cannot go forward as it should, until we are all willing to work in harmony and peace with all men."

Photo 1.1 Graduation day, May 1928

Another part of the application process concerned references and recommendations from individuals who had known Adelaide from church activities, and personal friends. A few examples illustrate their opinions of her readiness to be a missionary and her personality.

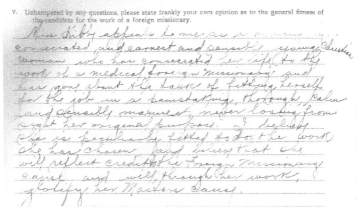

Photo 1.2 From reference form submitted by George White, family friend
(Courtesy of Presbyterian Historical Society archives)

Photo 1.3 Comments by Mrs. A. A. Brown, member of St. John's Presbyterian Church
and Sunday School teacher (Courtesy of Presbyterian Historical Society archives)

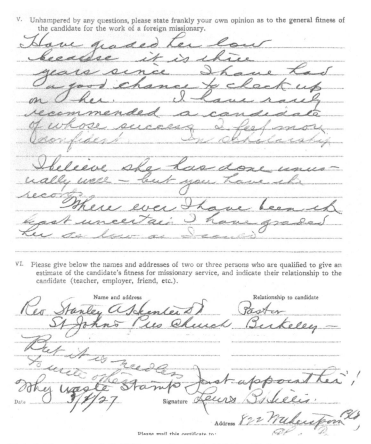

Photo 1.4 Suggestion by L B. Hillis, acquainted with Adelaide while Student Pastor at UC Berkeley (Courtesy of the Presbyterian Historical Society)

Photo 1.5 Adelaide Kibbe about 1928, prior to assignment as a missionary

One of the supporting churches was the Chinese Presbyterian Church of Oakland, California, which had been established by her Grandfather, Rev. Ira M. Condit, as part of his Home Mission work with the Chinese on the west coast, after his five years as a missionary in Canton, China.

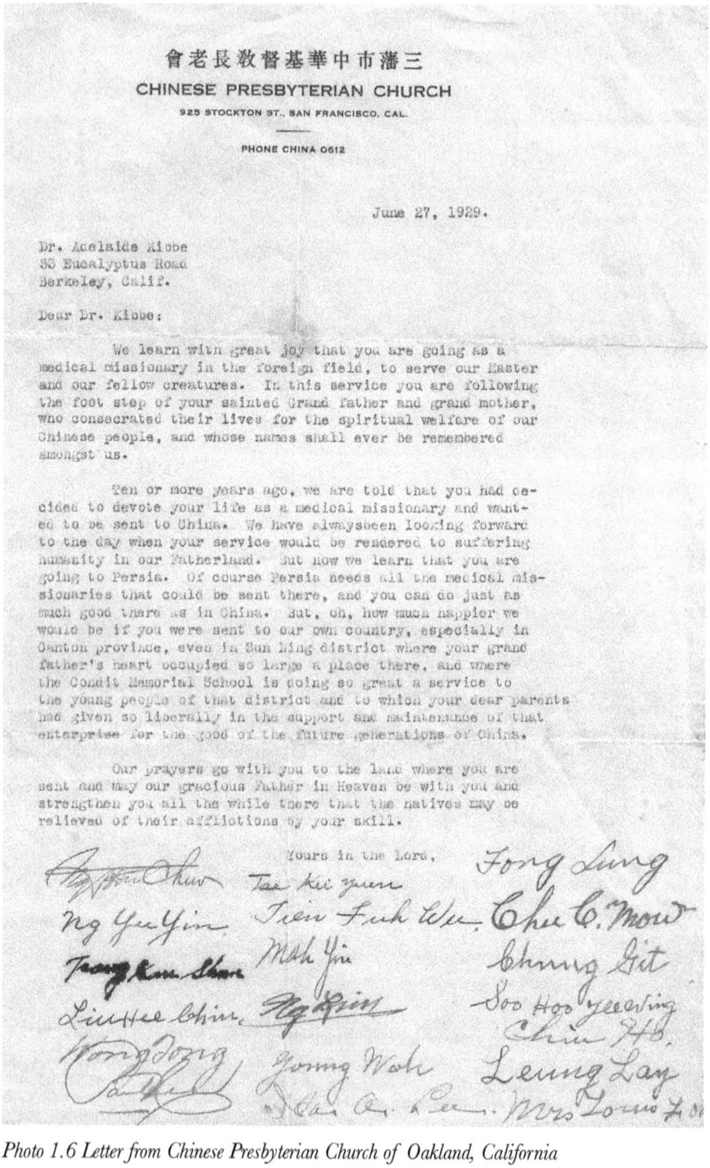

三藩市中華基督教長老會

CHINESE PRESBYTERIAN CHURCH

925 STOCKTON ST., SAN FRANCISCO, CAL.

PHONE CHINA 0612

June 27, 1929.

Dr. Adelaide Kibbe
33 Eucalyptus Road
Berkeley, Calif.

Dear Dr. Kibbe:

We learn with great joy that you are going as a
medical missionary in the foreign field, to serve our Master
and our fellow creatures. In this service you are following
the foot step of your sainted Grand father and grand mother,
who consecrated their lives for the spiritual welfare of our
Chinese people, and whose names shall ever be remembered
amongst us.

Ten or more years ago, we are told that you had decided to devote your life as a medical missionary and wanted to be sent to China. We have always been looking forward
to the day when your service would be rendered to suffering
humanity in our Fatherland. But now we learn that you are
going to Persia. Of course Persia needs all the medical missionaries that could be sent there, and you can do just as
much good there as in China. But, oh, how much happier we
would be if you were sent to our own country, especially in
Canton province, even in Sun Ning district where your grand
father's heart occupied so large a place there, and where
the Condit Memorial School is doing so great a service to
the young people of that district and to which your dear parents
had given so liberally in the support and maintenance of that
enterprise for the good of the future generations of China.

Our prayers go with you to the land where you are
sent and may our gracious Father in Heaven be with you and
strengthen you all the while there that the natives may be
relieved of their afflictions by your skill.

Yours in the Lord,

[handwritten signatures:]
Fong Lung
Tse Kei Yuen
Ng Yee Yim
Tien Fuk Wu
Chee C. Mow
Fong Kee Shon
Mah Yin
Chung Git
Lin Hee Chin
Ng Kim
Soo Hoo Yee Ving
Chin Fo.
Wong Tong
Yong Wah
Leung Lay
Pau
Dea A. Lee
Mrs Louis F.

Photo 1.6 Letter from Chinese Presbyterian Church of Oakland, California

Diary entry July 15 1929:
"We waved goodbye this evening to my dear father and brother, and a group of friends at 1st and Broadway. My heart is full – too full for speech. How thankful I am for Mother's comforting presence."

My grandmother, Nellie Condit Kibbe, traveled out to Iran with Adelaide and the two of them enjoyed visiting and sightseeing through England, Scandinavia, Germany, Switzerland and Egypt on the way to Persia. My grandmother was going on to China to visit her own birthplace, and the church her father, Rev. Ira M. Condit, had started in Canton. After a few weeks helping my mother settle in, she traveled by train across Afghanistan to India where she could get a boat to China, and then on across the Pacific back to California.

The Salutations of the Dawn

Listen to the exhortation of the Dawn!

Look to this Day!

For it is life, the very Life of Life

In its brief course be all the

Varieties and Realities of your existence:

The Bliss of Growth

The Glory of Action

The Splendor of Beauty.

For Yesterday is but a dream,

And tomorrow is only a Vision

But today well lived makes

Every Yesterday a Dream of Happiness,

And every tomorrow a Vision of Hope.

Look well, therefore, to this Day!

Such is the Salutation of the Dawn

Iman, Words in Pain, 1919
(Frontispiece from the Sanskrit)

CHAPTER 2

Trip out to Iran

THE LONG PLANNED JOURNEY TO IRAN
BEGINS WITH SEA TRAVEL

American Merchant Lines
S.S. American Banker
July 28, 1929
(3rd day out)

Dearest Webster family[2],

    The water all around us is such a heavenly blue, there's a fresh breeze outside, and the ship isn't rocking or rolling much this morning. Though we have all the time in the world I haven't gotten down to writing any letters yet! I do so love to sit in my steamer chair and read or snooze or watch the water. Up on deck is surely

---

the best place to be, but one can't write letters there very comfortably.

To go back to events in the past, we finally arrived safely in New York City glad of clean beds and a bath and sleep after our long journeys though we did enjoy it all. The Monday before we sailed we spent in Washington D.C. I was very glad to see it all, though I was fairly dizzy from gazing so rapidly at the 'sights'. In N.Y., we rushed rapidly from Board Rooms to stores, back to hotel and to stores again, and so on, until we finally came to the bottom of our list. And then came the great day – our day of sailing. After we had passed the Statue of Liberty and the New York skyline had faded from view and we could see only water around us, then we went down to our cabin and were glad to find and read all the nice steamer letters, telegrams, packages, and enjoy the flowers, too. Letters are the best ever and brought you closer to us than anything else ever could. And from now on we will have to depend on them.

And what have we been doing on shipboard? I like best being up on deck in the breezes – or walking for exercise. That and reading form our main occupation, pleasantly broken, of course, by meals – plenty of 'em and enjoyed too! The waiter told me I'd gain weight by the time I reached London. I felt quite indignant because I have been leaving out several of the seven courses, more or less! We like the boat very much, though we would appreciate a cabin a bit larger and with a bath. The boat, as we may have told you, is smaller than the big liners, carries freight and only about 74 passengers – has no jazz band (though someone is playing a miserable record on the Victrola this instant) and people do not dress, and there seems to be a nice crowd.

Nothing very exciting has happened – saw a school of porpoises and others have seen sharks and flying fish! The loveliest time of day is in the evening when we sit in our cabins and watch the stars come out, and get brighter as the day fades. We haven't been seasick yet, though we are not bragging!

Ad

Photo 2.1 Adelaide and her mother, Nellie, on board

FIRST STOP IS IN ENGLAND

Imperial Hotel, London, England

August 5, 1929

A Bank Holiday and today we ventured out in a London holiday crowd. We haven't been able to get in touch yet with our tour people (holiday, of course) and so we stepped out on our own hook. Took a bus for the zoological gardens and Regent's Park – tuppence a piece – (figure that out!) and a shilling to enter the park. When we first went in there was a pleasant crowd there – so many little children. I do love the English children, rosy and cute, but really I never saw homelier mamas and papas – a rather nice looking girl when she smiles has the worst teeth or else none at all, or all false. I'd say England needs a dental campaign among the middle classes. To return to the park and the excited children – munching peanuts, pushing and pulling each other to see the monkeys first. I adore the boys with their round caps, short trousers, socks, and little coats. We saw nearly every animal under the sun – the homeliest hippopotamus ever, a huge rhino that opened his ugly mouth for peanuts, and Mother's pet, a wart hog, positively the ugliest thing ever created with skin that looks, as Mother said, like pineapple skin or a cactus plant! Giraffes, lions, bears, zebras, and so on. Beautiful colored birds, pheasants and the daintiest, salmon pink herons standing so solemnly on one foot, and a serious looking penguin.

Two things impressed me – considering the crowds there, and it increased towards afternoon – the place remained orderly and clean, though every bench was filled with picnickers eating snitches out of a paper bag, and second the nice clean cages of the animals – many of them with center grass plots and shrubs around all beautifully kept.

We decided to buy a little something and sit in the sun to eat and gaze at the lovely flower beds and herons. Eight pence for four bananas was easy to manage – then we wanted some cookies or chocolate – a package labeled 'rocks' looked interesting but didn't say whether it was candy or cookies. We asked and the girls said they were 'rocks'*. We inquired if they were cookies –

"No," she said. "Rocks."

"Candy?"

"No, rocks."

"Well, what are rocks?"

"Rocks!"

Finally another clerk said, "Sweets".

So we took some chocolate and were glad to move on. Half the time we can't understand what is said to us. What'll it be like in Sweden?!

Then we walked thru Regent's Park – passed beautiful flower beds – full of all kinds of old fashioned flowers, but arranged to bring out the color. Then another bus ride home – though not so directly as we hoped for we didn't know which way to turn and got balled up – after asking three or four people we finally took a taxi (nine pence) and found it wasn't very far. And that's today.

Dearest love to all six,
Ad

* Candy made in a long brightly colored cylinder

Imperial Hotel, London, England
August 9, 1929

Dearest Father and Harmon[3],

Tuesday morning we left early in our big comfortable char-a-banc along with about 20 other people, driving out through South West London, (and such traffic in these narrow streets) through the peaceful, green country to the little old church called Stoke Poges, built in 1100 – and still used. Here in the graveyard Gray is buried, and they showed us the stone bench under the immense yew tree where he wrote his elegy – about the 'winter flannels of the poor'. Then on down the winding road to the Thames River at Boulton locks. We didn't realize what was in store for us. Soon a little sightseeing launch came along – we all piled in, went through the lock, and were off down the river. I was quite delighted by the way the green lawns and gardens came right down to the water's edge, the lovely old estates, or even just the fields with many fishermen along the banks, a few ducks and swans in more quiet places. We passed through three locks and then saw ahead of us the towers of Windsor Castle, after an hour and half's ride. Soon we turned a sharp curve (the river is very winding here) and came up to the town of Windsor, the castle on one side of the river and Eton College on the other. We were taken to a house for lunch – built and lived in by Sir Christopher Wren in 1667 – and how good the hot soup, roast beef and peas, and plum tart tasted (better than most English food, I might add). After we were warmed and refreshed, we walked up the

---

3   Adelaide's brother

hill to the castle. Can't describe this old pile – it is very extensive, beautifully situated on a hill looking over the valley of the Thames. We were only shown, of course, certain rooms and were nowhere near those of 'our sovereigns'. We saw mostly the State Rooms and those given over to visiting kings.

First we came to an 'armory' – up a broad staircase at the top of which the visiting royalty is met by the King. Here is where the armor of Henry VIII (he must have been short and fat), of Charles I, and his brother Prince Henry is kept – all beautifully polished, one inlaid with gold – and many spears, swords, lances, and so on. Then on to the rooms, one after another – magnificently furnished of course – silk brocade on the walls and covering the furniture of rose or in another room, green – old master pieces on the walls, beautiful vases, priceless pieces of furniture. In the long banquet room called King George's room – where are found on the walls all the coat of arms and their names of the knights of the Garter, from Edward III to the present. In the Queen's Presence Chamber and Audience Chamber were beautiful old Gobelin tapestries illustrating the story of Esther. After all this splendor, and more too, we went into a small room where is the Queen's Dolls' House, a most interesting miniature house with every conceivable article from actual linen on shelves to a lawnmower in the yard. This was made by expert workmen ex-soldiers – hired by the Queen, for which she paid 250,000[4]. It's quite a remarkable thing for its completeness of detail.

We were sorry to find Saint George's Chapel closed, so left the castle and went over to Eton. There one of

---

4   Monetary unit not identified, mostly likely in pounds

the school room keepers showed us the old school room built in the 15th century by Henry VI and still used. The benches are so marked with names and carved up, and the whole thing so worn, that one realizes that it's not for the beauty of the place that the Earls and Lords send their sons there. He showed us, too, the hall, stairway and two rooms all covered with names of the boys who had been students there. After leaving Eton we drove back toward London coming finally to Hampton Court Palace - another huge structure of red brick - built by old Cardinal Wolsey - lived in by Henry the VIII and other Kings down to William and Mary, none since then. We only had time to walk through the great courts and into the beautiful formal gardens and enjoy the lovely flower beds - the English do have an effective way of combining colors and getting a beautiful mixture of flowers. We felt we had had a most interesting day despite the fact that it had poured rain most every minute!

Yesterday we went shopping - London has fine, large stores - Liberty's is beautiful, we liked Peter Robinson's best. Think I shall say goodnight and finish this tomorrow.

8 a.m. Monday

Well, we have enjoyed London despite the rain and some difficulties in getting around it, both of which were to be expected. The English are very polite and on the whole helpful and kind to us - though we do have a terrible time understanding them! We are gradually getting on to the British currency, too.

To you both,

Ad

ON TO THE CONTINENT AND A COMPARISON OF
EUROPEAN COUNTRIES

Stockholm
August 27, 1929

Dear Father and Harmon,

Another step in our seven league boots and we are in Sweden.

Mother will tell you of the trip to Bergen (a nightmare, now that we have experienced sea sickness) and the lovely little town of Bergen, the beautiful ride thru the mountains across Norway to Oslo – just like an all day's ride in the loveliest and wildest parts of the Sierras – snow fields, granite rocks, trees (evergreens) and fjords with noble mountains rising from them.

We arrived in Oslo about 9:30 in a very hard rainstorm, and wonder of wonders were actually 'met and assisted in transfer to our hotel' – which hasn't happened so far. The hotel didn't prove to be much of a hotel – smelled of whale oil! But we only stayed there two nights and a day. Oslo has some fine public buildings (but not comparable to those of Sweden in beauty and number). The most interesting sights of the morning were the 'open-air' museum of folk history, the old Viking ship, and the place where the great ski meets are held.

The open-air museum is a large park and in it are these old buildings illustrating the history of Norwegian life. First we saw an old 'Stone' church built in the 12th Century – all of wood and curiously carved on the inside – outside of typical old Norwegian architecture with roof curving up gently at the edges and decorated with dragons at the corners. Not a piece of metal in the building, around it is a porch where amour and such were to be left before entering.

Then came the 'rich, country gentleman's house' of the 17th century – presented by a wealthy Norwegian – one room except for a small guest room, with two wooden beds – high sides and short in length (the Norwegians sat up in bed with many pillows and only rested their legs!). The large main room had a long solid oak table and benches, two similar beds, a fireplace in one corner, windows, and a large cabinet of carved wood, also fine old pewter plates and copper kettles. This house was shown in contrast to a typical home of the 15th century with no windows, central fireplace – open – with a crane (pulley) over it, wooden dishes, similar beds though. Also saw 'steam bath house' where one crawled in a low door, into the small room where a large fire was kept going. They stayed in these until they were good and hot and perspiring and then rushed out and rolled in the snow – the cure for everything.

The old Viking ship is carefully preserved in a simple building built expressly for it. This old ship was found buried in the earth a few years ago and was dug out, fixed and put here. Built in the 700s for Queen Ose – her pleasure ship, and the ship in which she was buried along with an old cart, four horses, one bull and twenty doves to help show her the way to heaven. It is 63 x 16 ft. and is the well-known shape – like a duck – the stern of her is broken off. It had one mast and about twelve oars. It has to be kept at a temperature of about 42° F or it will fall apart!

Early Monday morning we left Oslo on the train (2nd class coach) for Stockholm, first to Charlottensberg, the border town of Sweden – where the customs man came along – he stood in the door and rattled off something in Swedish, which neither of us understood though Mother says she heard the words "cigaretten and cigars" – we looked blank and shook our heads and he passed on – easy, I'd say. Then came the passport man and alien cards to fill out, and we were in Sweden. Norway is beautiful for her natural scenery – we just loved it, but Sweden is surely more progressive and up to date than any country so far. We marvel and wonder and admire, and finally rave about Stockholm. It's a marvelous city – such beautiful buildings I never did see – lovely parks and walks – these picturesque canals and the lake – old and new and very modern. Far ahead of anything in England!! In fact we like Sweden much better than England! Hotels, railroad trains, and especially the food – delicious food in both Norway and Sweden which we didn't find anywhere in Great Britain. They just can't cook there. Anyone who travels in Europe and misses Sweden and Norway (and we will probably feel the same about Copenhagen) surely misses a beautiful capital city and the loveliest mountains. This morning we had a most interesting drive around Stockholm. I hardly feel equal to describing the fine public buildings of this city – its broad streets, many bridges and rivers (in the city), and the general effect of efficient management and artistic construction. I shall only mention a few of the buildings – 3 huge stone museums, a new and really beautiful Polytechnical Institute – red brick and lovely green lawns, very extensive buildings, fine ship building offices (one, Johnson a shipping magnate, building is shaped at the top like a ship) elegant apartment houses, the King's Palace, the Parliament

Houses, and churches, and last the most beautiful city hall – completed a few years ago. Really this city hall is most beautiful building I was ever in – simple, but elegant and enormous.

And, of course, there's a smell of tar and fish around the boats (many of them tied up along the streets) and every other person has been a sailor, I suppose! But that doesn't mean there aren't fine looking men and women on the streets, better than in England, perhaps!

Must stop some time, much love to you two dear ones. You must come to Scandinavia.

It's worth being seasick.

Ad

During their travels in Europe they flew one leg on a Junker Trimotor Lufthansa flight. When my mother was feeling rather airsick the man sitting next to her offered her brandy to help calm her stomach. That just made it worse. For the rest of her life she commented that she could remember the smell of the gentleman's extremely strong aftershave.

Geneva, Switzerland
Sunday, September 15, 1929

Dearest Father and Harmon,

As you wondered – Harmon – if your letter smelled of paint, so I wonder if this has the aroma of horses! For we have just returned from a stately and dignified ride in a carriage of some nationality – brougham, I guess – around the city and a pleasant ride it was too, for an hour. We thought it quite fun to move slowly, for once...

This morning we walked up the hill through the quaint narrow street of that part of the city, to the old cathedral of the Reformation – St. Peters. We walked home down the little narrow street, no sidewalk at all – where [John] Calvin lived and died – passed a house where George Eliot had lived, and down finally to the river and the bridges. Geneva is a very pretty city. The old historic part with narrow winding streets, old houses of stone, each with its balcony – or flower box – and the modern new part, the eight fine bridges across the Rhone as it emerges from Lake Geneva – the harbor – the promenade on three sides of it and fine palaces, hotels, and public buildings.

The town is full now with the League in session and national flags fly from all hotels. It seems strange not to see the Stars and Stripes among them[5]. At our hotel are the Japanese and the German delegations and fine looking men they are, too, as we see them in the dining room.

Having begun backwards and told of Geneva I shall now jump across the Lake and tell of Montreux. Montreux is a perfectly delightful place and I should like to go back there someday. Tuesday when we arrived after a very hot and dusty ride across France, the coolness and freshness of the air, the lovely blue lake with background of mountain – all jagged and toothed in outline but no snow visible that day – were so refreshing and restful.

The next day we took a motorboat ride of half an hour over to the old Castle of Chillon. A fine old place, well preserved and restored, the rooms furnished with

---

5   The United States did not join the League of Nations

fine carved wood furniture and chests, old pewter, and so on. We saw the dungeon where St. Bonnivard was a prisoner – and the many passages and tunnels – as well as the spacious rooms of the Duc de Savoie. I rather like this old castle and believe it was in better condition and much prettier than any we have seen.

We felt we would like a view of the Alps if we could only get one, so at the suggestion of the hotel porter, we took the funicular Rail Road which leaves Montreux several times a day and runs up the mountainside – passed several hotels and resorts and on and on up with pretty steep grades – through ten or eleven tunnels and finally ends on the top of a mountain 6700 ft. high. There is a nice hotel and back of the hotel a short climb to a point where we had our wish – a wonderful panorama of alpine peaks – glorious jagged snowy peaks and great glaciers, so many in view that day, for they said it was unusually clear. We could see the Jungfrau – and south of it with many noble peaks in between – Mount Blanc – then turning around there lay Lake Geneva and Montreux, Vevey, and Lausanne below us. Then we felt we had really seen a bit of Switzerland and were content to leave. An old Swiss codger up there – who let us look thru a telescope and glasses – gave us all of a piece of Edelweiss, so we even have that!

Good night and best love and a big kiss from,
Adelaide

**ABOARD A SHIP FOR THE FINAL TIME
AND A SIDE TRIP TO THE PYRAMIDS**

S.S. Champollions
September 19, 1929

Dear Laura,

This is late morning, just after breakfast of tea, orange and ½ roll, and this is the first line I have written since coming aboard. We found the young people on board – four girls and two men who scatter after reaching Beirut to several different points, two into Persia beside Adelaide. Both short-term teachers – one a lovely girl from Wells College, which sends a representative for three-year term constantly. The other I forgot to count – she sits aloof from the group. It does not look well for her future work. The others are a gay set – modern young people – the men smokers, one a good musician, who after his three years are up, returns to begin his theological studies. The Mediterranean Sea is smooth and beautifully blue. Rev. Y. A. Trull of the Board is here also, and his son, 15 years old. Mr. Trull is on a long tour of inspection of the stations to study various aspects of the work – to be gone almost a year. One important matter I mention now. A letter on board for Ad from Miss Stephen of the Board said a cablegram (came) from Mable Nelson of Meshed to Ad received in N.Y. said, 'Very hearty welcome', so I took that as an official announcement that the East Persia Mission at its annual meeting in August had decided that Ad should be assigned there. She was disappointed at first, but took it calmly and thinks it will be good, but not as interesting a place to live as the capital city. It means an added three days journey by automobile to Meshed and the carrying on of all her boxes, trunks and twenty packages of books. It will necessitate getting cots and bedding for the nights on the way. I almost feel like backing out myself, but how can I when this near the goal. I find too that there may be a more direct route homeward from Meshed by auto to a railroad terminus in Beloochistan, across India to Calcutta, then by steamer to Hong Kong. I cannot find out more until I reach Beirut.

Today about 1:00 p.m. we reach Alexandria, found our steamer waits 48 hours, and we can go south to Cairo and get a glimpse of the pyramids – we hope to do that.

So goodbye for the present.

Sept. 23

We did go by train to Cairo, and spent the night there. The next morning we took a trip with an Arab guide, who spoke good English, and gave quite a lecture on the many objects in the museum, where one large hall has only the things from King Tut's tomb – jars, table, canes, boat, beds, jewelry, beautiful vases, and boxes of alabaster.

Later in the day we rode out to the pyramids along a road lined with acacia trees beginning to bloom with big red flowers, with the Sphinx not far away. We climbed up a few steps of Cheops, rode a camel to the Sphinx and meditated on our death! The guide took us to an old deserted palace where we had a fine view of the city, an old roman aqueduct, the distant pyramids at Memphis and minarets nearby. Afterwards, we visited the Alabaster Mosque built by Mohammed Ali, where his tomb is, and saw an old carved screen. We went down a little ways the into the square excavation in solid rock called Josephus well, and saw water glistening 385 feet below. It took us three and a half hours to make the trip to the pyramids, made interesting by watching the agriculture – cotton fields, ripe Egyptian corn in tassel, rice, potatoes, date palms, and crossing the great Nile.

Tuesday – we reached Beirut this noon, but it was a slow process getting all the formalities over. Finally we landed in rowboats for 100 yards, perhaps, there are no piers but one. A missionary met us and did the arranging, and another one brought us by auto to our cool comfortable hotel. Tomorrow we go to Damascus, stay there all night, then start to cross the Syrian desert – 36 hours, day and night – hot, too...

Must close, goodbye dear ones,
Mother (Nellie)

CROSSING THE DESERT INTO PERSIA

September 25, 1929

Dearest Father and Harmon,

Just a note to add to Mother's before we begin the next step when we may not have much chance to write. It does seem like a thrilling adventure to us four – especially as yesterday Mr. Erdman said he just got word that there was fighting at the Persian border and we might have trouble getting into Persia – may have to stay in Baghdad for a few days, or possibly go by airplane – worse luck! We also have to be inoculated today for

Photo 2.2 Camel ride to the Sphinx

plague – a Persian requirement – here's hoping we aren't all sick on the desert ride.

Yesterday after finally getting through the red tape of landing, baggage and customs, and so on, and we settled in our hotel with a late, but welcome lunch. Mr. Erdman called for us in his Ford (new one) and took us to make arrangements for the trip. They find you can save three quarters of the total by going in a private car rather than in the Nairn Stage. We would all prefer to go in the big comfortable stage, of course, but the matter of cost must be considered – so a seven passenger private car (a Buick – 1929 – by the way!) it will be – the four of us and all our baggage (10 pieces – two of them trunks) in there for a 36 hour ride – no stop for the night! Guess we can live through it though. We go today to pay for it and fix it all up! We sat in the chairs and talked it all over, through Mr. Erdman speaking in Arabic to the headman. We leave tomorrow morning for Damascus – stay there all day and night and leave early Friday morning. We are buying goggles and scarves for our heads, and so on, for comfort on the trip and will have a bag or small basket for little articles.

The heat does continue – and that sun is hot! Mother seems to be standing it all very well. And she is not discouraged by the news that I am to go, probably, to Meshed instead of Teheran. This means three days longer journey from Teheran and more difficulties for her to get into India, so that I almost hesitate to have her try it.

Time for Mr. Erdman to come now so I must put on my hat.

Goodbye,
Adelaide

Photo 2.3 Seven passenger 1929 Buick. (Photograph retrieved from www.imcdb.org, originally appeared in the 1935 movie, Danger Ahead.)

Baghdad, Iraq
Sunday, September 29, 1929

Dear Ones,

    The desert trip is over. I'm thankful to say we are still alive and fairly clean again. Our driver after many false turnings found the Y.M.C.A. where Mr. Lamphart has given us two double rooms with sitting room between. It is a building with a courtyard, dust colored ground, and four or five date palms. A garden opposite would be pretty if not laden with dust. Everything seems to have that coating. We would not care to live here. We left Beirut Thursday the 26th, Ad's birthday, at 10 o'clock with our party of four, all the luggage strapped outside and a box of ice with bottles of water and various baskets and bundles – our lunch and melons, inside, three of us in the back seat, and one in front. From Beirut to Damascus it was interesting, over hills terraced and planted in vines, villages clustered frequently as we looked over Beirut beautifully situated, the Mediterranean Sea blue as lapis lazuli – so we enjoyed it – down Lebanon mountains, across a plateau with Mount Herman looming on our right – reaching Damascus about 1:00 – the hotel (best one) made us wish they would use soap and water everywhere. We found a guide right at hand and he took us to see an Industrial Exhibition for a short time – fine textiles, brocades, inlaid furniture, brass tiles, easily all made in Damascus. Then we walked by one mosque, which had a series of rooms all along an outside wall, each covered with a dome – the effect was of a collection of bulbs piled close, the other mosque was much older, away back to heathen Rome, Theodosius, finally became a Mohammedan mosque. We walked through the bazaars, took a carriage – little low wheeled affair, and rode in the street straight to Saint Paul's window, ruins of the house of Arminias, and along streets, crowded and dirty. We decided we never wished to reside there.

The next morning we started early in theory, but the men again had trouble tying on the luggage. All day we were on the desert – at first a bunch of grass, then small tufts of grass, then nothing but gravel in spots, and earth yellowish brown, not real sand. After several hours we all stopped at a small enclosed place, about 10 or 11 cars in the convoy. We drank water, ate a few grapes while they examined our passports – on again – not exactly a road, but the driver choosing the best looking spots – but bumps and dust, clouds and clouds of it. Sometimes two or three cars would get quite close try to pass and then the dust was trebled, sometimes we kept abreast yet far enough apart to avoid that. About 2:00 p.m. we gathered together again and tried to eat, the cheese we didn't like, but eggs and fruit tasted well. About dark we came to the Oasis so called, no trees, but an Inn, where the driver allowed us an hour. At 2:30 a.m. we reached Ramani – a tiny place, but with a 'New Babylon hotel' – and the driver announced he would not leave until 4:00. We sat down to a table with tea, oranges and eggs, but could not eat the other greasy food, wandered about in the old moonlight, laughed softly not to disturb the Arabs who all seemed to sleep strewn about the machines. Just before 4:00 the customs men banged about, for this was Iraq, and we showed our passports again. Finally off we started – more desert, camels again approached – some loaded and in trains, some grazing – donkeys and more. At length we crossed the Tigris, and stopped at the outskirts of a real city, Baghdad. All the luggage was unstrapped, opened, questions asked, and reloaded – the driver was quite proud of doing the trip in 23 hours, 520 miles. We finally found the Y.M.C.A., where Mr. Lamphart gave us a kindly practical welcome.

All morning we have been busy – getting money changed from Syrian and English into rupees, and a little Persian – also hired an automobile and man to drive us clear to Teheran, after we spend this night on a train where we can sleep and rest while he takes the trunks, meeting us at the rail head tomorrow. At Teheran the two girls will be finished, but Ad and I have three days more to Meshed. It was 105° yesterday and seems hotter today. Persia will be cooler and the mountains very much lower in temperature...

Much love,
Nellie

THE LAST PART OF THE TRIP CROSSING
PERSIA TO MESHED

Meshed, Persia
October 14, 1929

Dear Verne and Harmon,

We are here and nearly across to the eastern boundary of Persia. Ad's journey is ended and mine half done.

On Monday evening, Mr. Lamphard saw us off (from Baghdad) on the train at 9:30 p.m. – we four had a train compartment, (rented) bedding, and slept very well. This train also stopped at long intervals, its speed about 20 miles an hour, naturally we were late instead of 5:00 a.m. arrived at 7:00 a.m. The man we had engaged, 'Long Jack', had driven the 130 miles with our baggage, met us here, and ordered breakfast – canned fish and porridge. We started out soon, crossing the border into Persia – passports out and certificates of inoculation. The head man sent word to come in for refreshment. It was soda water, bottled, and fans to use while we waited. He bowed us in and out most politely. For seven miles the road was paved, thereafter always dusty and generally rutted. The camels passed us loaded, more often the donkeys carrying straw or alfalfa stacked above their little heads or wood or bags of earth or rocks for mending the roads. We passed villages of mud houses, sometimes a ditch of water flowing in front or behind the houses next to the road – stopping at Tea Houses where tea was drunk from a glass or cup, and where we ate an apple or an egg. We finally came to Kermanshah, had dinner (first a hot bath) and slept in their lovely guest room, and in the morning visited the mission hospital where Dr. Packard works. Another day of travel the same kinds of scenery – arid, dusty – road often full of donkeys – camels and sheep – gardens, sometimes patches of vegetables. We climbed a pass, 8250 ft. still no verdure or trees. That night in Hamadan Ad felt pretty sick from her inoculation, feverish, hives. All the following day she and Miss Browne were miserable, joints painful, each had symptoms. Thursday evening at dusk we drove into Teheran. By Tuesday, we had rested some and decided it was wise, according to the others advice, to go by airplane to Meshed, which did not leave till Friday. The flight was supposed to be five hours but it was seven and not very pleasant – stopping once on the way. Mabel Nelson and Miss Reynolds met us with two *droshkys* (carriages) and took us to the Rev. and Mrs. Miller's home, who have a large unused room, where we are comfortable and treated with kindness.

With love,
Nellie.

Home

Desert sands and mountain height,
Valleys green and cities bright,
All the breadth of ocean blue
Lie between my work and you.

But when my sun of afternoon
Strikes light upon the hills at home,
I know full well you wake to say,
"God bless the one so far away."

And when my Persian stars shine bright
On the still loveliness of night,
I know 'ere long they'll watch you pray
God's peace upon my dawning day.

O souls so true! O faith so blest!
In your dear prayers I find my rest;
Nor homeless I, though far I roam;
In your hearts' love I keep my home.

By Annie Woodman Stocking (Boyce)
Written in 1919 on her arrival in Persia

CHAPTER 3

Settling In 1929—1932

The first few years in Iran Adelaide kept a diary and journal of her impressions and feelings. As her life got busier the entries became fewer and fewer. The first part of this chapter is excerpts from those sources.

EARLY IMPRESSIONS OF MESHED

"Then came Meshed and getting acquainted with my own new home place. A dusty city with high mud walls, queer narrow crooked streets, little shops – so many men, and children in all manner of costume and a few women in their black *chaddors* (veil). Donkeys everywhere – occasionally a dignified camel or two – *droshkys* bumping along – the costumes are numerous here in a busy Meshed street – only a few of the old *abbas* (men's cloak), many tall Afghans with their white turbans, Kurds usually in colorful dress, over all gleams the golden dome of the great and sacred shrine to the Imam, its two minarets and the beautiful blue dome of the mosque.

A cloudless blue sky, a warm sun and the cool air of late October, in the distance the wrinkled, furrowed hills, barren and treeless but lovely against a sunset sky.

An afternoon ride, and on another occasion a walk, revealed some of the beauty of this country of Persia:

- trees of orchards in lovely golden yellow colors with their white silvery bark or gnarled old fruit trees
- orchards surrounded by the high mud walls
- a walk along a stream under trees and thru a carpet of yellow leaves beneath which the winter wheat is sprouting back as the sun is setting and hills reflect the lovely colors (Meshed is on a broad plateau)
- long camel trains are coming in to load up the night's caravan of freight

We reach our compound and are glad to be safely inside it and back in our comfortable homes.

On our famous camel ride and picnic 'twas dark before we got back and a lovely moon, a huge yellow moon, rose up over the hills and lighted our road.

At night we can hear the coyotes or jackals howling outside the city wall and early in the a.m. the camel bells as the trains start out and later *muezzin* (*mullah*) call from his minaret."

SUNDAY AFTERNOON WALK

"Through narrow streets, in and out, and around and finally arrived at a courtyard gate! There we visited one of the hospital men, his wife and baby. We all sat under their *kursi* – a pan of charcoal, with a frame over it and then covered with large blanket, other blankets and pillows around it for warmth and comfort. We had the usual tea. Then on to the main avenue, where we met a friend of Mabel's who dragged us down narrow *kuchis* (alleys) to her home. We saw them weaving a rug, climbed a ladder to a roof of one of the houses and from there could look into the Shrine hospital garden, which is rather barren now. Next we passed the mill in the middle of the avenue where they have harnessed the water supply to turn their two mill wheels to grind the wheat. We said '*mashallah*' (Allah's blessing) so that we wouldn't give their stones the evil eye. At a rug factory, we saw such wee children working with their deft, rapid fingers. One is still rather a curiosity on the streets and the men all stare quite openly and often laugh after you have passed."

Dec 15, 1929:
"A very icy day. The trees covered with frozen snow are like a vast and irregular orchard in spring blossom, a beautiful sight. We can't see our mountains for the clouds, but they are in a white blanket, too."

DELIVERY CASES

"My first one in Persia – in hospital and in bed. All went well until I sneezed and Mabel said I must sneeze twice or the baby would have to wait until I did!

Delivered baby out under the trees with only some sponges, cotton, my medical bag and two forceps, all went well. Incidentally I was on my vacation and only had a piece of store twine with me."

PERSIAN TEA PARTY

"Outside the gate, down a narrow street, into a courtyard and up very steep high narrow stairs – there in a pleasant west room where we gathered, sat on the floor on cushions, a cloth spread on the floor and on it many small dishes of *shirini* – cakes, nuts and candy. Tea was served in glasses with aluminum spoons. Then some singing and dancing to the Persian music. The drum played by one of the women and tambourine-like instrument, acting out a story – more tea to drink. Then we said goodbye. I tried to say a few words which always causes much merriment!"

VISIT TO A LEPER VILLAGE

"Sunday afternoon a group of us drove out in *droshkys* to the village outside the city wall and across the fields. A group met us at the gate and spread the news we were coming. They seemed glad to see us and followed us around, a large and curious crowd. They were so delighted with the flowers taken out to them and one old man with only a button for a nose kept holding his two chrysanthemums up to his nose, as though he loved their pungency. They seemed happy and contented there, the children giggled and laughed as any would. Their little rooms are quite clean and neat. A few pitiful blind cases will probably not last the winter. Quite a different place than one might expect a leper village to be."

PATIENT'S COMMENTS

"Give me some medicine for I haven't sneezed for
two months."

"(I) put manure on sores and places of pain."

"Not yawned for 20 days since eye sore."

" My nose itches" – main complaint.

CLINIC PATIENTS

"Many patients want more children and haven't had any
for months or years. What can I do? They think I should
give them *bacheh's* (children)"

"A hospital patient admired my red rubber gloves. I told
her it was rubber but Dr. Lichwardt said it was pigskin!
She drew her hand away in horror and said, 'God forbid'!
Poor dear, she will have to go to the bath and say many
prayers unless I convince her it wasn't."

"Mastoidectomy on son of a religious man – the father
stayed in the room part of the time, praying, and holding
the Koran wrapped in a cloth over his head as the
anesthetic was given."

"An old woman started out on a pilgrimage to Meshed from
Yezd, broke leg by fall from camel two days out, rode for 40
days to get here on camel with her broken leg."

"Baby 30 days old came in with abscess of whole back
and pus coming out of neck. Fell out of bed two or three
days before and hit back on corner of wall. Now almost
gangrenous – very foul. Died after a few days."

"Woman in labor ten days – fetus heart not heard (11th baby). Baby finally born alive with forceps!"

"Patient with turquoise set in front gold tooth had whole row of gold teeth. Another patient stripped off her gold tooth (covering over good tooth just for looks) and offered it to me!"

"One day early on I went on hospital rounds with Dr. Blair and into a private room where the father of the patient was in attendance. He was in his voluminous stripped cotton underpants and shirt – no trousers or hat or shoes. I was all for backing out but Dr. Blair urged me on saying it was perfectly proper. The man made a dive for the nearby cupboard and I expected to see him emerge in proper dress-pants, but he appeared as was with his hat on. It is very improper and impolite to appear before a lady without your hat!"

MY FIRST CONSULTATION CALL

"We were requested to consult on the wife of a big official, Bir Jand. Mabel and I went in style and dignity in the *droshky* – down the center of a narrow street. We left the *droshky* at the door and went on through two large courtyards to the women's quarters, up narrow steep stone stairs to her room. It was a large room with a *kursi* on one end near the windows and a stove and table with two or three straight chairs in the other end. The patient – a nice woman of 35 or so – sat under the *kursi* not acutely ill. A Russian midwife who had attended her previously was also there. After tea and talk over the patients history I did a pelvic exam in due deliberation. Then Dr. Hoffman came and her own family doctor. They climbed in under the *kursi*. Later we retired to another room and talked her over. One of the numerous servants flitting around brought in a brass bowl and graceful pitcher with a long narrow spout from which we poured warm water over our hands – also, had bars of soap and a towel. The next day Dr. Hoffman and I went for another consult. Three doctors – the two of us and a Russian doctor – and the midwife decided an operation should be done and we are wondering if we will see it. She had probably an ovarian cyst. (We didn't do it!)"

SUCH AN INTERESTING FAMILY THIS

"Father and Mother pretty staunch Moslems – wealthy, of good position, the father clings to his *abba*.

1st Son – a hospital *mirza* (learned man) and a Christian.

2nd Son – also a *mirza* and goes itinerating with Dr. Miller, unpaid, to speak for Christ.

3rd Son – city health doctor, has studied in Germany and such a fine appearing man. He helped his younger brother when the family turned him out. Tried to make an enemy like him and love him."

MOHAMMEDAN CUSTOMS

"Woman, postpartum, on 8th day if a boy and 10th day if a girl <u>must</u> go to the bath regardless, or say prayer for one year until she has another baby; the baby is taken along and dipped into hot water seven times, Mohammed said so."

"Don't praise a new baby but call it ugly – so it won't have the evil eye on it."

"Little girls age nine onwards are married."

"Baths in the hospital – patients won't allow themselves to be sponged off or bathed – have persuaded them to take a 'shower bath' by pouring water over them."

"All running water is pure and water of certain amount as in a *hose* (pool) of certain size is pure! It is used for everything and in the *jubes* (ditch) all animals and man use the water regardless because it is running."

"*Ramadan* fasting – can't even swallow their spittal during the fast; they eat after sun-down."

"Husband and wife must walk together on street or ride in carriage now. Yet, she may still walk behind and he in front, and can, in Teheran ride together and in most occasions do."

"Woman gets out of the way of the man if passing on the street."

"Married woman can see only her father, husband, and brothers of her men folk."

"Many charms fastened on sleeve or around neck to protect from the evil eye mostly, few for good luck, some for disease – different kinds – and some to make people love you."

"Rabbit flesh will bring babies, if eaten, to a woman without them."

"Walk under a camel and eat camel's flesh so your baby will be born all right and come soon."

"*Ramadan*: girls at 9 and boys 15 must fast (also considered marriage age)."

MOURNING CALL

"On the third day after death of Allia K's brother, all the mourners were seated on the floor around the room. We were greeted by Allia as we entered, she crying aloud and moaning. All were dressed in their black *chaddors*. In the center were the following: the cloth from coffin cover, on it were four lighted lamps and at either end two large boxes leaning against which were two mirrors – on them his picture, also Korans along with a green silk cover wrapping up some object – perhaps his clothes – in dishes were henna, apples, sugar."

LETTERS HOME DESCRIBING DAILY LIFE

Meshed, Persia
October 20,1929

My dear Dr. and Mrs. Hunter[6],

Your letter and enclosures of September came this week. How exciting it is to get letters out here. Glad to hear the Loyalty Campaign is encouraging. You were very kind to write to me.

Now that we have actually reached Meshed, and language study has officially begun, I feel as though I really was a fledgling missionary. A fledgling because without the language or someone to interpret I am not of very much use. And every day I see there is so much to learn of national customs, of methods of work in a busy, busy hospital where supplies are precious, and of how to adjust one's manner of living in a new country, that really I cannot object to being called the 'baby of the station'.

Of course you want to know how it feels to be away off here and how I like it and what I think of Persia, and Meshed, and my work in particular. Ten days is hardly sufficient time for one to have formed ideas of any value. But I did want you to know my first impressions and also to know that I do hope that I can keep St. John's church interested and thrilled over the work here, feeling that through me, as their representative, they actually have a share in healing and caring for the sick in body and soul. And as for there being raw material here – if they could only come and see, they could not help but give of time, money and self.

---

6   Pastor of her home church in Berkeley, California,
           St. John's Presbyterian

I was, indeed surprised to learn that Meshed was to be my station instead of Teheran – perhaps a bit disappointed at first. But now that I am here, have become acquainted with the fine families here and the two single women, have seen the hospital and the compound and met some of the Persian Christians, I feel I am very fortunate, and perhaps find it an easier place to start in than the capital city. Anyhow, I am mighty glad to be here and I know I shall love it.

Surely a few days ride through the country and a visit to a few Oriental cities is a wise preparation for coming to your own city! For in comparison with some, the beggars, the dirt and dust and disease didn't stand out so startlingly when we dropped down in our aeroplane from Teheran as it would had we come directly from Berkeley, California! That is my first impression of Persia and, in fact, the whole country from Alexandria to Meshed! My second is this: that water and care and a few seeds can do wonders. Flowers and grass do grow beautifully in our missionaries' garden and in those of some of the Persian families. The gardens in our compound are a great delight to me, even though with winter coming on they are not at their best. The desert can be made to blossom.

Then, after seeing the compound, came the hospital. Directly after landing and removing the dust of travel we went to the hospital. Never have I felt quite so touched, so humble, and so proud, too, as I walked through the hospital for the first time. The whole place had been scrubbed and washed and cleaned and put in order 'for the new lady doctor who is coming', from the pharmacy storeroom with shining bottles and orderly shelves, to the polished linoleum floor of the operating room, to the hospital wards and patients themselves. Even the three old washer women were so excited, that when they saw us coming they rushed to put on their brand new flowered *house-chaddors* and came back smiling and bowing and saying *salaams* (greetings) in true, polite Persian manner. And so the word has been going around that a lady doctor is coming and the women are glad and do you wonder that I feel so? The two doctors tell me that I can eventually begin any kind of work or clinics that I want to and feel necessary. I think there are vast and interesting possibilities ahead, *when* I learn the language.

Therefore as winter comes, and by the way, it gets really *cold* here with snow and heavy winds, as well as hot in the summer, I shall be trying to say, 'How are you feeling today, and what is your pain, and the ball is under the table, and so on.' and perhaps soon learning to read those queer chicken tracks! The Persians like to have you try to talk to them and we all laugh over my attempts. They have a good sense of humor among their other characteristics.

Missionary life has proved most interesting so far – rounds of teas, dinners, and lunches, all informal, of course, the first station meeting, church school on Friday and Sunday services, and even a camel ride and picnic, and a visit to the bazar.

Paper and time are about used up, and I haven't even mentioned the poor clinic folk, their half-starved, filthy, diseased condition – with an occasional well dressed, really clean person. So many are penniless, homeless pilgrims, for Meshed is, as you may know, the Holy City of Persia – for here is a very sacred shrine. And we can see it from here, through the trees and the flat mud-roofed houses – a great golden dome with two golden minarets, shining in the sun light, and to one side the turquoise blue dome of the great mosque. Meshed, on the border of Afghanistan, India, Russia and Turkestan, is an important city and a most needy one.

Yours sincerely,
Adelaide Kibbe

Sunday Evening
November 3, 1929

Dearest Harmon and Father,

We know it is November here for the air is quite nippy towards evening and in the mornings the grass is covered with frost. The flowers are dying off, except the chrysanthemums and they are lovely, the trees are turning lovely yellow gold colors (rarely are any red) and losing their leaves. And pumpkin pies are being served here and there, so it must be fall. Our fire in the wood stove tonight feels mighty comfortable.

So several weeks have gone by since last I wrote you. Now it's Harmon's birthday and soon it will be Thanksgiving. And someone said today that we should soon be getting our Xmas letters and cards off to America! Harmon dear, I hope you have been having a happy day – we have thought about you, and wished that it might be so. It's 6:30 here, so I suppose it isn't even quite noontime with you.

The days have slipped by rather fast and they have been busy ones too, at least the hours seem well occupied. This is my schedule now – for the past week since I acquired two more teachers.

Lesson	7:30 to 8:15 or 8:30
Breakfast	
Lesson	9:00 to 10:00
Hospital	10:00 to nearly lunchtime at 12:30 or 1:00 three days a week dispensary three days operating

After lunch I have been studying or making rounds in the hospital wards until 2:30

Lesson	2:30 to 3:30 or 4:00

From four our recreation, tea, shopping, tennis (!) and so on – dinner comes late and then some studying and bed rather early.

So far, we have had a party or two and other dinners, and so on, as I mentioned before. Last Thursday we, Mabel Nelson – with my humble assistance – gave a Halloween party and had lots of fun. Bobbed for apples – stunts and so on, and ended up with apples and nuts, candy, pumpkin pies and tea. We do invite the English people – more or less – and go to their homes in return. This week I have been asked for dinners and that means evening clothes, which I haven't with me unfortunately.

While speaking of parties, yesterday Mabel had a few of the Persian women and girls in for tea and stunts. We all sat on the floor (I may learn to, yet) and after tea had some native music – one instrument was a drum held in the lap and played with the fingers, very clever and not easy to get the rhythm, they say. And the others were two round things that looked like tambourines only two or three times as large. They were played by moving them in rhythm and the noise came from many small metal rings tacked on the rim inside. The girls sang – I don't 'understand' as yet, or 'appreciate' Persian singing, however! But their dancing was good – really graceful pretty steps, as I watched I felt it would probably make quite a hit on the American stage!

Language study is getting a good start now, with my three lessons – though I can't say I speak fluently yet – and I am having quite a time learning the script and printed script – that and the <u>verbs</u> are my special bugbears now. The Persians take great delight in trying to help me learn the language and speak to them. They all want to have their share of teaching me a new word or two and are so tickled when I say 'goodbye' or '*salaam alecum*' or 'thank you', and so on, in my halting fashion. One of my teachers is a young girl and we converse together (she speaks no English) – the next is a young man who knows some English and teaches in our boys school. He sticks more to grammar and the hateful verbs and in the afternoon comes the old Sheikh Moabali – who has taught most of the missionaries out here. We read together and converse too – he does most of the talking, however, and I spend my time trying to recognize a word or two.

Today has been a lovely Sunday – two services this morning and after dinner Mabel, Mother and I took a long walk across the fields (green with new crop of winter wheat) and down a narrow road between high walls and then around several vineyards and over walls (I got lost and couldn't get out, too) and back by a main highway out of Meshed to our gate in the city wall. A lovely walk, though, with the autumn colors and keen air.

Ad

Meshed, Persia
November 24

Mother dear,

Somehow ever since you left I seem to have a lump in my throat, whether it is a sore throat or something else, I am not so sure! But I do know this that it seems very lonely without you – as though something very near and dear had dropped out of my life and I am entirely alone, now. But of course, I am not all alone, and that feeling will go soon, I hope. I realize more than ever how very fortunate and happy a thing it was to have you here – for by now I am better acquainted and feel a little as though I belonged. I hope you will never regret coming – surely they all loved to have you here and all of them have said how dear you were and how much they enjoyed your being here. So you did good to them, to me and I hope to yourself!

Very often I think of you riding along Persia's dusty roads and I do wonder if you are comfortable, all of you, and if you especially, are not finding it too hard. You are such an all-around good sport that we feel satisfied everything will go nicely.

When you get this little note, I suppose much of India, new scenes and new faces will be behind you. And I shall be so interested to hear your impressions of India and of those whom you meet there, how it compares with Persia.

Yesterday afternoon after a bath and clean clothes, I went with Mabel to this English girl's for tea. In the evening I read a bit downstairs with the Millers. Today nothing unusual has happened – except that we had a new and very delicious *pilow* (rice dish) for dinner which I do wish you could have had – rice with a few carrots, blanched almonds, and a little berry or currant-like thing with a cranberry taste – and the whole sweetened. It was delicious!

Well, I believe I will not move over to my new room until I have time to go to the bazaar and buy a lamp and few things – probably about Wednesday I will carry my belongings across the road. Tomorrow comes the wedding or I would be ready by Tuesday. I am really thankful you all left yesterday instead of today, for now the weather is much colder, suddenly, and a storm is brewing somewhere. This will be old history to you when you get this.

You will be pleased to hear that I have been, already, attempting to fix up my diary! You see you have more influence on your wayward daughter than you think.

I did want to kiss you goodbye again – oh, several times, but I know I couldn't do it and not weep – so I didn't. I suppose they thought me hard-hearted. But I don't care as long as you know that I do love you and long to be worthy of your love for me – and of being your daughter. Someday maybe I will be.

Goodbye, Mother dear, and much love following you, as you go farther and farther away from me towards home.

Adelaide

Meshed
Tuesday Evening

The mail doesn't leave here for India until Thursday, so I kept the letter and will add a note.

The next excitement (after Thanksgiving) will be welcoming Mr. Steiner back and hearing about the trip. I wonder if you are arriving tonight in Duzdap and what tomorrow will hold for you as you try to make train arrangements.

Today I have been thinking about furniture and wish that you were here to help me plan it. I have decided to try to follow the picture in the *Good Housekeeping*, if possible. The carpenter is going to see if he can find enough pieces of wood with a pretty grain to use for the chest of drawers and bed. They will be plain except for the grain as you may remember. If he can't find them I will choose another style. Also we bought a lamp – a real good oil burner with a circular wick, brass standard and green glass shade! The standard is quite pretty and someday I can have a pretty shade made, for company. So my household articles are increasing. Oh yes, I bought a pitcher, bowl and soap dish of enamel. Tomorrow I believe I will move – if all goes well – the room is ready with washstand, bed made up, closet ready, a small wardrobe effect with shelves for my clothes, and everything in readiness.

I miss you so much and wish you were going the other direction! How scattered our family is now – for Thanksgiving and X-mas both! Nan Hahdi sent her *salaams* – many of them, to you – she points to your bed and sighs and says something and then points to heaven! Even the carpenter asked for you! A big kiss and hug from,

Ad

Winter 1929

A snow storm in Persia, with the wind howling outside our window, snowflakes fluttering and blowing, and best of all, a roaring fire within and warmth. Does that sound like Persia to you? Or does this, ice every morning in my water jar in my room? It is not Persia as I expected it to be, either. Yet they all assure me that someday I really will need the sun helmet which I bought in Baghdad.

Meshed, here in the northern part of Persia, is in a fairly broad valley, 3000 feet high with hills and mountains up to 10,000 feet, on either side, now white with snow. Russia and Turkestan are not far to the north of us, and Afghanistan to the east. And for at least two months more we will have real winter weather which means hard times for the poor people with little food, fewer clothes, and not much for fuel. I feel so sorry for them I am ashamed to complain much of the cold which I am not used to. But, it is fun to bundle up and go for a walk, or for a ride in a *droshky* (our taxis). The Persian boys in our school have learned to really play in the snow and make snowmen and have regular snowball fights. But snow means such awful mud later, as soon as the sun comes out, the narrow streets are ankle deep in mud, and the patients come in with wet shoes, and mud-splashed *chaddors*...

Christmas day was such a full one; after our regular morning duties, we had the English service. Then, following a turkey dinner, came the Persian service, tea and Christmas tree, and in the evening an annual event, the dinner at the British Consul General for all of us. New Year's day we women were at home to our Persian friends who cared to call, and they did, all classes of them, over 300 not counting some of the children, were served tea and cakes, and shown pictures of the Christmas story.

Nearly every day some interesting event happens, and I always think I would like to tell my friends about it. These are only a few thoughts after my first three months in Persia. It is a most satisfying life being a missionary, and you may be sure we don't work all the time, but have fun and good times, too!

My best greetings and love to you all,
Adelaide

December 29, 1929 – January 2, 1930

Dearest Family,

When we are so widely separated much 'supposing' is necessary – so I suppose as I write, you are recovering from your New Year's celebration, whatever that may have been, and I suppose, that when you get this letter one of you perhaps both (!?) will be gone to meet Mother in the Hawaiian Islands. Another difficulty and unsatisfactory thing about letters is trying to get questions answered. So I have made a list of your inquiries in all your letters since October, herewith send the answers!

Thanks for –
1) Your Christmas telegram greeting in a very unexpected and most happily received evidence of your love and thoughtfulness.

2) Your pictures, which are <u>splendid</u> and I am awfully pleased to have them and am very proud of my two handsome men folk! They came thru safely and in good condition along with a batch of Christmas mail on Christmas Eve.

3) The paper telling of the fire – interesting to hear but rather tragic news.

4) The two batches of Medical pamphlets. They are a problem to know what to do with. Will they keep on coming until Doomsday? Out of the pile a few are worth reading or keeping and the blotters are handy! However out here they may become of more value and if it isn't too much trouble you might keep on sending them for a while, anyhow.

5) The phonograph records which are on the way – somewhere. I shall be quite thrilled to have more. My first boxes arrived two or three weeks ago, containing phonograph, typewriter, and odd things. And the phonograph has already become a great joy and I love the records you picked out for me. Any will be very acceptable for our tastes are similar.

6) Your many nice letters which have come along quite steadily – except for two written in October which were two months getting here after some which were written a month later, and explained a long silence.

Miscellaneous –
1) Mail: I understand from various ones that it isn't necessary to put 'via Berlin or Kiev' on the letters, that

most first class mail comes that way anyhow. Also, I guess second, third, and Parcel Post, does have to go via India and Duzdap - at least it all seems to arrive from there. Packages, if small and slipped into an envelope, are sent best via first class, if larger Parcel Post is better, protected if necessary by a box. Often, I see they come several in gunny sacking or cloth and sealed. Mails are not to be trusted way too much in this country - packages are often delayed a month in some little town. Duzdap is the worst offender - or Karachi.

2) A Sunday paper once in-awhile would be quite interesting and fun to peruse. I do feel rather 'out of the world' here despite magazines regularly. The station is small enough and compact enough so that magazines are sent 'around' from one house to the next to be read and enjoyed by all. A nice system, too. We have a gateman who also runs errands for the station, goes to the bank, carries notes, brings our mail in, and so on. He comes to each house every a.m. for letters to be mailed, notes, and errands to be done. Quite a convenience, necessity really in our mode of life here - no telephones, or streetcars, no easy means of communication and getting from one side of the city to the other.

Now, I believe that covers most everything except Harmon 's questions about the country, living conditions, and so on. I'll tell you about that and then you can ask Mother to describe it all to you, too! Of course I don't know quite all about Persia yet, but I can describe a bit as I have seen it.

Let's see, first Meshed is a sacred shrine city, place of burial of the 12th Immam and therefore is a place for pilgrimage, about 100,000 steady population and as much more floating pilgrims from all over Persia – men, women and children – who have come weeks journeys on camel or donkey or on foot to visit the shrine. And too, located as it is not far from Russia, from Afghanistan, Turkistan, India and other countries to the north, there are many different nationalities to be seen on the streets.

It is situated on a dusty plain between two mountain ranges – valley of a small river – about 15 miles wide (I'm not sure of this). The nearer mountains are not so very high, but higher more rugged and jagged peaks are behind them. We are about 3300 ft. high here and the mountains rise to about 10,000 feet or less. Now they are snow covered and the higher ones glorious in the first morning sunlight or evening colors of sunset. They are, of course, barren and treeless, but one soon finds they have charm and are never the same color but the lights and shadows are always changing. We can see them so well from our living room, or better by going out on the roof (typical flat mud roof). Also one sees on the horizon groups of trees from the many orchards round about, also poplars and plane trees, which are quite common. For trees, grain, flowers can be made to grow if they are first cared for and watered. I am eagerly awaiting springtime, when orchards are in bloom, fields green, flowers coming up. They say it is lovely. The opium poppy fields are a beautiful sight too, though one hates to think of misery they cause. Now it is a typical winter scene – rather dreary, leafless trees, bare fields, frost killed grass and shrubs in the garden, patches of snow that has not melted. At least it isn't sooty from factory smoke!

Also, climate – I can say that ever since we arrived in October it has been cold some time during the day!

And for the last two or three weeks it has been frightfully cold – around zero every morning – and not going above 21° F for a week at a time – a little warmer now – the sun comes out and it is a bit warmer at noon if you are in the sun. I feel it more because the houses are not heated except for a wood stove in one or two rooms where we live most. That means our bedrooms are cold and I don't stay there any longer than I can help. There is ice in my pitcher and glass and *kuzeh* (water jar) every morning. I pile on the bedcovers and have even succumbed to a hot water bag. Whenever we go out in a *droshky* we take along a robe for our laps and put on all the sweaters and coats and scarfs we can find. Next winter I am going to have a fur coat and fur-lined coat! I though Persia was too warm for a fur coat but I've changed my mind! Also I am going to have some warm dresses and sox and sweaters. Everyone wears several layers! I guess they really have almost as much cool or cold weather as warm – say middle of October, it begins, to middle of April and varies each year, of course. Not much rain so far – one or two days with real rain, two or three snowstorms, and once it was quite misty which is unusual.

My boxes actually arrived this week and today I opened them up. I was informed that one had been pilfered before reaching Kermanshah. I find someone removed one of the lovely new pillows, a box of medicines (what they will do with them I can't imagine) and what is worse all the stuff that Miss Bryant was sending to Hamadan – about $26 worth of mentholatum, paring knives, soap, shoes, meat grinders, and so on! I wonder if they knew what it was all for and are grinding up the soap and cutting and eating the mentholatum as they sit on my pillow! The microscope was in that box, which they didn't want, but somewhere it had been opened and the door was left open and box not put back in its cleats but just jolting around. I wonder if it will work OK. I sent a letter of values and articles lost and will get insurance, I judge. I guess I didn't fare as badly as I might have – am sorry for the Hamadan folk, though! They will get money instead of mentholatum and paring knives this time!

I haven't had time to unpack yet and see if pictures and breakable things arrived safely. It is good to see my own belongings again and bring back 'home' rather poignantly.

It's getting late and the fire is dying down and I will have to pay extra on this letter if I write much more. I did mean to tell about Christmas – a busy time it has been. The day before – a big dinner for some 60 German refugees from cruel Bolshevik Russia and a service following the dinner with tree, program and music and food; wrapping presents for our Persian friends and the usual Christmas Eve excitement. Christmas day first came breakfast with the Donaldsons and our presents – then hospital rounds, a tea given by one of the hospital nurses, then English service, a turkey dinner, Persian service and tree, and at the different homes for our Persian Christians. We had the young boys and had a lot of fun. Then came getting dressed in our best for a big dinner at the British consulate General – followed by amateur dramatics which I was in – first time I ever did that and I really enjoyed it. Supper there ended our Christmas day! More teas, dinners, and parties and yesterday our all day New Year's 'at home' to the Persian women – over 300 – so we have been busy with all of this and lessons, occasionally Hospital. Now comes real study and oh, so many letters. I hope to compose a letter and make copies of it to save time.

Enough for tonight. I wonder when you will be a united family again with Mother back.

Much love and good wishes for 1930,
Adelaide

Photo 3.1 Mabel Nelson, Dr. Rolla Hoffman, Dr. Adelaide Kibbe with Meshed hospital staff, 1930

TYPICAL DAY AT THE HOSPITAL

STATION LETTER FROM MESHED, EAST PERSIA
MISSION SPRING 1930

Meshed, Persia
January 11, 1930

Dear Friends,

I have often thought, as I go to our 15-minute morning prayer service in the hospital – what a different group we have from that in any hospital at home. How spruce the internes, the nurses, and other hospital attendants were in their starchy white uniforms and, what's more, would the 'chiefs' sit down to read and pray with the cook and doorman? We gather in the men's waiting room. As we enter, one *farosh* (servant), the big black man, is tending the fire; he is a man of fine physique, black beard, black eyes, dark skin, and still a Mohammedan. With him is the other *farosh* with henna dyed beard, (the Persians do love henna and even the horses are jaunty with hennaed tails and manes!). The male nurses and *mirzas* come in, the head *mirza* a small man, rather dapper in appearance (and an excellent worker), then the cook with white apron, and his two helpers, lanky youths in blue denim smocks, followed by the pharmacist. Next the wash women and the scrub women in *chaddors* just alike, the women nurses in their blue *chaddors* come hurrying in, and our two Armenian nurses, and we four Americans make up the staff. Truly a motley crew!

Not all Christians, yet, but all faithful in attendance, and the Christians are always willing to pray if asked. One of our more educated women nurses led prayers one day, probably the first woman ever to preside in a mixed group in Meshed. And so we begin the day in our hospital.

But my day has begun before this, for my first hour of language lessons is at 6:30 (two hours more come later in the day). My sheikh – I wish I could describe him adequately! – about the homeliest man I ever saw, thin, and rather pathetic. Someone called him a 'picked chicken', and the description does fit him! But he is very dignified, a learned man, and he does know the Persian language. All of the missionaries have 'grown up' under his tutelage.

Clinic days I have been working with the women, and now I am planning to fix up my own office, and try to understand and to make myself understood, still a rather difficult task. If only they all had diseases as easy to cure as the woman who came in complaining that she had not sneezed for two months! And clinic days are busy days, though less so in winter, and I wonder if the time will ever come when I can see 100 to 150 patients in a morning, enough to stagger any busy clinic in America! The record for one morning was 250 or more. The clinics both open the eyes and rend the heart, not alone the diseases and the tragic neglect of human life, or the dirty children, or the many half-staved patients. If many in America could visit our clinic for only half a day, they would never say, 'Oh, their religion is good enough for them, let them alone' – not if they have any love for humanity in them. There must be more than that to help these people to good health, to better, cleaner lives, to joy in a life that is free from the dread of superstition.

However, not all of our patients are poor. I had the thrill on my first consultation call of going to see the wife of a prominent and wealthy man from a neighboring city, herself a princess. I went in due style and dignity, with Miss Nelson and the *farosh* to accompany me. At their home, after passing through two courtyards and going up two flights of steep stone stairs, Miss Nelson and I entered the women's quarters, where we found our patient. She was sitting comfortably under her *kursi*, (a pan of charcoal on the floor, covered over with a large comforter) and apparently was not very ill. After a leisurely cup of the inevitable tea, a discussion of the history of the case and an examination of the patient, the head of the Shrine hospital who is her own family doctor, and I talked it over. The whole affair took about two hours, an interesting morning's visit! Rather a contrast to a hurried house call. And thus I earned my first five *tomans* ($5.00) for the hospital.

The people are loveable, and our Christian group is a fine one. I am humble as I see them living lives loyal to Jesus Christ despite the difficulties, dangers and stigma of associating with infidels. They say it is only in the last few years that occasionally Mohammedans are willing to come into our meetings to listen to the Gospel of Jesus Christ. Thus does the father of one of our private patients (who only a few days ago held the Koran wrapped in a silk handkerchief over the boy's head as he was going under the anesthesia) come to our Sunday morning open service, and this week daily for our week of prayer. It is a great experience to be present when a Persian is baptized a Christian.

These are only a few thoughts after my first three months in Persia.

Sincerely,
Adelaide

Photo 3.2 Afternoon tea time and visiting

PERSIAN RELIGIOUS AND SOCIAL CUSTOMS

Meshed, Persia
February 19, 1930

My dear friends all,

How would you like to all really 'fast' this month of *Ramadan*, or our February. If you did fast in the proper Mohammedan manner you would lead a most topsy-turvy life, for practically speaking, day becomes night and night day. The *tupe* or cannon is shot off at sunset, that is after the sun has really gone down behind our mountains, watched by men waiting on the top of the minaret. Then one can hear a great shouting in the distance, all over the city, prayers are said, and one can make out several different calls to prayer, as they carry through the clear evening air. Then they have their first meal since sunrise, the first taste of any food, even water. After this many go to the shrine to hear talks by the *mullahs*, more prayers, and roaming around the mosque; or perhaps they go to a party or call on their friends. Some sleep part of the night, but they have to prepare, eat, and be all through their morning meal by the time the gun goes off at sunrise, now at about 5:00 a.m. And sunrise is when the first color comes in the sky and one can tell a black thread from a white one. Then, after this meal they crawl under their *kursis* and sleep until noon, providing they are not obliged to go somewhere, or the children don't wake them up! The sheikh arrives for my lesson every morning at 6:30 or 6:45 looking most woefully sleepy, for his night has probably been a busy one. Boys under 15 and girls under nine years do not have to fast (incidentally this is also considered the marriage age). And if the fast is strictly kept they can drink no water during the day, and must not even swallow their spittal. A patient in the clinic begged the doctor not to put anything in her mouth (he was painting her teeth with iodine) that would break her fast, for that means fasting another month. Now, do you think you would like to fast? A queer custom when you think about it, what is the difference whether you eat when the sun is shining and sleep at night, or whether you spend all night eating and sleep during the day? Why change day and night around and call it fasting and meritorious in the sight of God?

CUSTOMS AND PHRASES

One can think of a good many more things they ought to do, or not to do, that would surely receive more approbation than fasting, if only they could see it that way too. For instance the many superstitions – you must not praise a new baby, but call it ugly and say '*mashallah*', so that it won't get the 'evil eye', some to bring good luck, others to protect against diseases, or to hold the love of a husband. No baths except in a certain amount of water, for only running water, or this certain amount is pure. Imagine the foolishness of such a saying – all running water is pure – you would say it was more than foolish if you could see some of the streams in the city streets called 'pure'!

And it is queer to think that husband and wife cannot walk on the streets together or ride in the same carriage. She walks behind carrying the children. Though now more liberal ideas are coming in, they do occasionally ride in the same carriage. And suppose you were a married woman, veiled from all but your husband, father and brothers. When we have Persian women for a tea party, all the men folk must depart or keep out of sight, and only women servants are around.

As I learn more of the Persian language, I am particularly interested in a few of the odd phrases (yet are they so queer, we have odd ones of our own). Here are some of them:

- to fall down is to 'eat the dirt'
- to be sorry for a person is to 'eat sorrow'
- you 'draw' trouble or shame
- you 'draw' yourself out when you lie down

And if you would like a few pet polite phrases to show your own humility and the exalted state of someone else, here are two or three:

- 'your feet are on my eyes' – I am your slave
- 'bring your honoring to my humble abode'
- 'my hand is on your robe' – I have come to you for help

Or, if you are at party and are handed a cup of tea, you say:
- 'excuse me, may your hand never feel pain, your honor is great'

For someone who has been kind to you:
- 'may your shadow never grow less'

Two rather funny ones, try them on the next person who argues with you about money:
- 'don't waggle your chin anymore'
- tell them not to be confused and let their 'hands become feet!'

DAILY LIVING

And so the winter is passing, I am becoming accustomed to not hearing streetcars, automobile horns, factory whistles and the noise of the city. Instead we have the 'bath horns' tooting at most any hour to tell people the water is ready and hot! (And these public baths are a story all by themselves). There is the *droshky's* horn, or the drums from the minaret at sunrise and sunset, the call to prayer and someone singing their prayers, children shouting, dogs barking, or distant camel bells.

Yes, one does get used to living here in Meshed, different as it is from any place in America. But I doubt whether I will ever become hardened to hearing a donkey bray during church services, comparable to a fire engine, if not worse! I laugh yet when I think of it – six different times one Sunday morning during our service some donkey tethered outside, (I believe he must have had at least his head in a window or doorway), brought forth tremendous heehaws which echoed down the corridors of the hospital! And when a donkey brays, he does it in no uncertain voice, be he ever so little.

We are looking for signs of spring now, though it is only a little past the middle of February. Still the 'big forty days' are over, and the 'little forty' or twenty, are nearly gone, and then should come the rainy days, spring will really be here. Already we can find a few blades of grass, tender and green, and little new shoots are coming up where the sun has shown warm, melting the snow, and we have heard the song of a little spring bird in the air. Spring is on its way.

Sincerely,
Adelaide

SETTLING INTO DAILY LIFE

February 26, 1930

Dearest Home Folk,

My 'office' in the hospital is in working order now and I am attempting to see patients alone. However, it is still pretty hard for me to understand them and so get across my ideas, to work fast and not lose my composure! Certainly <u>language</u> is a terrible handicap to one's work. Also I am trying to fix up the lab – some cleaning, (removing) stains and getting it a little more shipshape. Language study continues daily, as usual. I am now reading John 14 (have read Chapter 1-14) and also a little child's primer! Which makes me feel a little infantile, but is about my stage of knowledge, I must admit.

Continued – Feb. 28

Now more snow and icy weather just when we thought spring was coming! Well, yesterday Mother's long waited for letter from Canton arrived written on the way to Japan. I am eagerly waiting the next installment, for the rest of the tale. How nice everyone was to you in Canton and I am sure you must have had a very happy time there – never to be forgotten. Yes, I too, feel, that our plan was well worth while and the trip a real success. Surely your part alone was not so bad, in fact, you got along very well, perhaps better! How's your health by now? You haven't said – so I'm wondering – no more malaria, I trust.

You asked, Mother, if I were living in the room downstairs. Yes, I am and am quite comfortably placed, I think. I will have to move sometime before summer though, as the Donaldsons want the room. Where, I don't know yet – but they will fix up some place, perhaps the room in the Steiner's house. I had my first piece of furniture, too, the chest of drawers (four drawers) of light walnut, very pretty grain – simple style – cute fat legs and curved lower border. Am now having bedside table made, same style and next will have a poster bed and dressing table. The chest cost 14 *tomans*, not bad for walnut. Really is very nice, I think. I have four rugs now! The Turkoman, the lovely old rug with the red colors and two small ones – both old – one lovely shades of green and blue with tan background and a sheen that is soft and beautiful, the other a heavier rug but rather pretty colors. It is a great temptation, indeed. I will try to get a few to take home, too!

Tonight the church is having a party for tea, games, and pictures, men and women separately, of course. This is their own idea and ought to prove a happy one.

Almost time to go to our regular Friday church school, and I guess I'll go out in the sun and try to get warm before the meeting. I'm frozen. After the meeting comes our prayer meeting for the women and after that tea at the Consulate and after that the party! Oh, there is always plenty doing around here!

Much love to you all and a kiss around the circle.

As ever,
Adelaide

IMPRESSIONS OF FIRST YEAR AS A DOCTOR AND MISSIONARY

Annual Personal Report
June 30, 1930

I have seen from the mountain pass Meshed's golden dome, beautiful in the plain below, the inspiration of all pilgrims, and have walked the city's narrow, dirty streets and met at every corner pitiful remnants of humanity, beggars, the despair of all Christians. I have heard the wailings and watched the ritual carried out in the home of the dead, and I have seen a gay party at the house of new bride. I have made *No Ruz* (New

Year is celebrated on March 21st) calls in the snow, rain and sunshine of uncertain March weather, to drink innumerable cups of tea.

I have watched the *Moharram*[7] procession, and seen with indignation the cutting of tiny babies' heads, the bloody ranks of professional head-cutters, the passion in the faces of the chest-beaters. I have sat at my desk in the clinic and given out advice as fast as I could, and on alternate days operated. I also have called in the homes, drunk the tea and *sharbat*, (fruit drink) and examined the sick one in dignity and leisure. I have risen at six winter and summer for my language lesson, and I have dined at the consulate. I have given thanks for the newly baptized Christian, and I have marveled at the power of Islam over its believers. Does all of this make one a missionary? Do I 'belong' yet?

Theoretically I am not, I don't belong to the Mission until that first year language examination is creditably over, and I can vote in station meeting. Practically I feel as though I do already belong, which is natural after the most friendly acceptance of my presence here in Meshed. But to go deeper than this, more than having entered into the life of a new country, its customs, its homes, more than having become acclimated and initiated into the new manner of living, more vital than these is the

---

7   *Moharram*, month of mourning, marks the anniversary of the Battle of Karbala when Imam Hussein ibn Ali, the grandson of the Islamic prophet Muhammad, and a Shia Imam, was killed by the forces of the second Umayyad caliph Yazid I. During *Moharram* there are *majalis* (gatherings) to review Islamic teachings and to commemorate Imam Hussain's sacrifice. The mourning processions include expressions of grief such as beating the chest, beating oneself with chains, and hitting oneself with swords or knives.

question of development of understanding, of sympathy, of the Christian attitude toward those for whom I am working. What have I learned, where do I stand, after the few months here?

I feel that I am in the process of revising my opinions about medical missionary work, for I, myself, am both the judge and the one judged, no one else. I was guilty of thinking before I came out here that medical work was the way to reach the hearts of the people, that it would be easy to speak of religion when a person is down and out, sick and suffering, that I could help to accomplish great things for Persia's womanhood. Are the people in the clinic whom I see in a hurried way, influenced, made aware of the love of Christ because I am a Christian doctor? Attempting in an all too imperfect way, to act as He would have me? I would like to think so. Again I am challenged by the progressive Persian men and women who are already beginning to raise the standards of prevention and treatment of disease for their own countrymen. How far can they go? Do they need our help, limited as we must be by personnel, funds and time? I shall reserve the right to question, and wait for the answers, recognizing my own weaknesses, at least until I have learned to express myself in Persian (Farsi).

Meshed Station Medical Report
Meshed 1930

For a doctor just beginning to practice, to start in such a hospital as we have here in Meshed is an unusual opportunity. You do not need to wait behind the new desk for the two or three new patients to come in, but as soon as you can say, "Where does it hurt and why", and understand some of the answers, you can sit in the clinic and see just as many as your time, strength, and language capabilities will allow! And as for surgery you can attempt anything from cataracts on down to amputating toes, especially if you are as fortunate as I have been to have two senior surgeons who are always willing to help me in my inexperience and lack of surgical judgment. However, I fully realize that I will only gradually become an asset rather than a liability to the hospital, in so far as I continue to study the language, and endeavor to develop a sympathetic understanding of the Persian mind and customs, as well as gain medical skill.

PUBLIC HEALTH

In these first eight months in Meshed, several as yet undeveloped projects for work in the future have presented themselves. First, a thing that was mentioned the very day I arrived, the training and teaching of the local midwives. These 'mamas' have not, of course, rushed to us eager for knowledge, but ready in the background with dirty herbs, or sticks, or fingers, as the case may require, a sinister menace to every woman. And when a poor woman is brought in, you know she is infected. If she gets well, and a surprising number do, you thank God and marvel, and if she dies you are again impressed with the necessity of a plan to give these midwives training. In parts of India a system of training, examining, and controlling these midwives is in good running order, with the help of the government.

We hope, in the near future, to begin some such system here, for it is as much needed in Persia as any oriental country. And with our new public health organization in the city, we ought to be able to accomplish far more than we ever could alone. But this requires money, which we have not at present.

Second, the little children of Persia. What a field lies here! Babies are brought to the clinic unwashed, joggled and carried all around, and fed every time a cry or laugh is heard, stuffed with tea or sweets or even cucumbers, or worse soothed with a 'bit' of opium from the day they are born. Little children, and skillful workers they are too, work all day from sunrise to sunset in a rug factory, or perhaps punching a bellows, for such a pitifully small sum, not enough food, no school or play or sunshine for them. And almost a hopeless task to help mothers, so often she will have none or only one or two living children out of eight or ten! One is baffled at every turn seemingly by some age-old superstition or Mohammedan custom, or the unfortunate limitations of extreme poverty. No use to say, "bathe your child daily," for they would have to take it to the bath, an impossible expense, and those baths are a menace in themselves. "Let it play and kick on the floor, don't wrap it up tight," only possible in summer because of the draughty cold floors. "Give it whole cow's milk, cereals, eggs, and vitamins from seven to nine months on," it would take more than a whole months wages to buy these 'luxuries' for one week in many families. A nursery connected with the hospital where the mother can remain and be taught the proper care of the child is a possibility, and has been successful elsewhere, however not without its difficulties, first of getting the mothers to come and then to carry out what they have learned after they leave.

The answer to the many medical and public health questions seems to me to lie in the religious convictions of the country, if the Quran sanctions it anything is permissible! We are only hitting our heads against a stone wall of Mohammedan law and superstition, unless we can eventually work from the inside out, the very center of their existence outward, we will never be able to help them to health of mind and body.

Adelaide Kibbe, M.D.
Appointed, 1929

TAKING MEDICAL WORK TO THE VILLAGES

STATION LETTER FROM MESHED, EAST PERSIA
MISSION FALL 1930

Meshed, Persia

Dear Friends,

What does the term 'medical itinerating' mean to you? Do you think at once of a doctor on horseback or astride a donkey, saddlebags filled with medical supplies, going from village to village and treating the sick as they gather around him in crowds? At least here in Persia the 'saddlebag doctor' has gone out of date as automobile roads come in, roads that make possible transporting supplies for a real hospital.

Medical itinerating is a semi-annual event, an undertaking that involves much planning beforehand, and preparation of enough supplies to last six weeks. A rather large staff of workers is necessary for efficient handling of the crowds who come. I went down two weeks after Dr. Hoffman and his staff had opened up at Nishapur, and found our hospital in good running order with plenty of work for all. They had taken over the whole of an old *caravanseri*, which seemed to be adaptable as a hospital in this country. It had many small rooms built around a large square courtyard. An old teahouse at one side of the entrance was made into an operating room suite, and upstairs, in front only, were our own living quarters.

DAILY SCHEDULE

In the six weeks spent there a tremendous amount of work was accomplished, for a day's schedule is a heavy one. After breakfast and prayers, at about 8 o'clock, come the morning rounds of the inpatients, and the clinic begins, for some patients will be waiting. I saw only the women and children. These *Nishapuris* are such a friendly people, mostly village folk, more so I believe than those in the city. They are always ready with a smile and interested in all that is going on. I enjoyed them all. After they had seen the doctor and gotten their medicines, they would drop into Miss Reynold's room or that of Schail (one of our Persian Christians) to hear them talk and read from the Bible. We saw all the patients we could until lunchtime, and about 2:30 we began operating. Though we hurried from one operation to the other we took time to enjoy the funny things that happened, for instance the patient who brought her own thread for her operation!

Also time was necessary every few minutes to shoo out the curious who strayed in our door to watch us operate.

STAYING IN THE HOSPITAL

Lack of space required several of our inpatients to occupy the same room. They brought their own comforter, samovar, food and utensils, if they had any, and along with them a 'few' relatives and friends. Entering their little rooms never failed to give me an indescribable feeling of pity, and hopelessness, that people could live in such a manner, for it was only too truly a reflection of their own homes. Yet more tragic than this, in Persia, is the young girl who because of some blemish is not eligible for marriage, and either is very poor or has no family at all, and consequently has absolutely no means of support. She has nothing to look forward to except being a beggar on the streets or worse. One longs to gather a few of these girls together, to create a home for them where they can learn some useful trade, and be shown what it is to live a happy clean life. What is wrong with the world and this country?

Sundays we had two services, one in the morning for general public, and in the evening for the Christians only. The morning service was held outside on the porch, rugs put in front for the men to sit on, and behind them the women gathered, benches for them if they cared to sit down. Such a group as sat there listening to Dr. Hoffman preach and read the Bible!

Cordially yours,
Adelaide Kibbe, (M.D.)

Photo 3.3 Helen, Rolla, Harriet and Betty Hoffman

STREET SCENES

STATION LETTER FROM MESHED, PERSIA MISSION,
SPRING 1931

Meshed, Persia

Dear Friends,

Take a walk with me outside our compound gate,
down this narrow little street with the rough cobblestones
and onto the new avenue, and see what December
brings to Meshed's thoroughfares. Even though the
air may be frosty and a sprinkle of snow on the distant
hills, the first thing we see is a little boy of perhaps four
years with nothing on except a thin short shirt, legs and
feet bare, but rosy cheeks, beneath the dirt, testify to a
healthy constitution. Survival of the fittest! We walk on
past fruit or food stores, their wares always arranged
in a symmetrical design and decorated with a few red
apples, paper flowers, or green melons. The keeper of the
store may be busy, but never frantically so, or he may be
leisurely sipping a cup of tea and indulging in a bit of
gossip with the usual collection of bystanders, warming
themselves over a pan of red coals. There, on the next
corner sits an old man of indeterminate years, with a
white beard that would be an addition to any Santa Claus
outfit, and spread out before him is a display of choice
articles, such a funny collection, odd buttons, old pieces
of broken china dishes, keys and nails of assorted sizes,
tops of teapots, cheap jewelry, and anything he may have
picked up. Someone bought a ring from such a 'bazaar'
and found it to be a passable diamond!

As we stand at the intersection of the new avenue and the old street with the stream of water in the center, which leads straight down to the shrine, we can watch the 'traffic'. Here comes a group of three or four Afghan men, tall, bearded, of fine physique, their full white, baggy trousers flapping as they walk, with white coats or possibly an old American army khaki coat, great white turbans, embroidered shoes with pointed, turned-up toes, and numerous silver finger rings. Occasionally their women folk are seen on the streets. They wear white *chaddors*, gathered into a cap, which covers the whole head and face and has a small strip of embroidery in front of their eyes. There goes a dignified, henna-whiskered *mullah* riding on his little fast-trotting donkey. He is still allowed to wear a turban, but the general laity must be seen only in their 'street-car conductor' hats. Black robed figures pass by, our Persian women, usually with a child or two in tow. A 'delivery boy' shuffles along carrying on his head a large wooden tray piled high with sweet cakes and candies for a tea party, or perhaps with a load of earthen ware water pots, or watermelons, or flat loaves of fresh bread. One always sees men with a small rug slung carelessly over their shoulder, an original form of advertising, and they are quick to notice anyone who may evidence any interest in it.

The water carrier passes, bearing on his shoulder a bulging, dripping goat or sheep skin, 'fur side inside', legs tied up, and the neck has become the spout! We turn around to see from whence comes the tempting smell of cooking meat, and see on the far corner a brazier of coals and a man cooking *kabobs*, much relished bits of broiled lamb or mutton, first cousin of the hot dog idea. "Hot potatoes, nice fresh hot potatoes!" is a frequent cry.

We step aside to allow a donkey train to pass, saddlebags loaded with new bricks, and from a side street we hear the deep bells of a camel caravan, headed toward the desert and a distant village. Carriage drivers shout their warnings to children playing in the road, village folk in picturesque dress stare at us curiously. And, by this time the ever-present beggars have surrounded us, trying to work on our sympathies.

My first year in Persia has passed, and winter is again in the offing. I have not found Persia to be all a garden of roses with nightingales singing, nor is it all beggars and dirt and disease, though after a busy clinic day one is tempted to believe the latter! But not all Persian women are illiterate, and it is refreshing to meet here a women who is intelligent, educated, cultivated, a potential leader of her sex. She may feel it is still necessary to veil her face, at least here in Meshed, but gradually Persia's womanhood will develop her own freedom, and that of her young girls.

Faithfully,
Adelaide Kibbe (M.D.)

Photo 3.4 Ad and Smoky, her donkey

Photo 3.5 Elizabeth Reynolds

CLINIC CONVERSATIONS

HOSPITAL STORIES FOR CHURCH NEWSLETTER

Meshed

March 12, 1931

"But doctor, you must give me an injection today, please do".

"Yes," says her husband, "my wife should have injections every day!"

"Oh *khanum, khanum* (lady)," I call, "don't put your clothes there, that is a stove and it is very hot!"

"May God give you long life, my hand is on your robe. I am a widow and have nothing. Please give me some really good medicine to rub on."

"We have brought her thirty miles on a donkey to see you. Yes, she has been lame for seven years. We can only stay three days and want you to cure her. Just give her some injections!"

"Nareh, if you want, let us operate on your eyelids now, you will become blind in a very short time. I will pull the tooth today that is bothering you, and you come tomorrow for the operation on your eyes. Yes, take one pill three times a day, and rub this medicine in thoroughly every night."

This is repeated five times before light begins to dawn, "This prescription doesn't belong to you at all, and it does make a difference. Where is your prescription? You don't need a separate one for every ailment."

"But she (she being at the determined age of two) won't let me wash her eyes, so I could not use your medicine."

"How many children have you had?" The reply is fourteen and one living!

"She ate some walnuts and this sore came out on her head."

Here I turn around to see whence the source of a sudden deepening noise directly behind me. One of the women in the room laughs, and explains that she has a chicken under her *chaddor* which she is taking home! And so it goes on all morning in the clinic, much to try one's patience, one's sympathies, and one's ingenuity and technical skill, not lacking however in the humorous side! I was particularly delighted by a poem written for me in the good old Persian style.

About the hardest task for me is trying to judge how much they can pay for operations and days spent in the hospital. This is an art, a matter of tact and insight to read the truth in their statements and determine a just amount for them to pay. Like human nature everywhere they will first try to get something for nothing. If that fails and you remain obdurate, then they try to bargain, to work on your sympathies, occasionally they go as far as to wear old clothes, and bring forth a hard luck story, concealing better garments beneath the ragged ones! This is what baffles me, not to say an unjust amount and drive them away with the idea that we are out for money, and yet not let them off too easy. I look forward to the time when we can find a Persian assistant, an honest trustworthy man who knows the Persian mind and logic, and can ferret out the true financial condition of our patients. As it is, some are undoubtedly turned away because the price is too high, and many others come in free, or practically so, who should be paying more for food and care. It is a delicate and difficult problem, and often we hear this: "Why, I thought you were Christians here, and you insist on my paying!" or "I am interested in Christianity you ought to take me in for nothing."

"Amed, Amed, she's come, she's come." This I hear as I look in on four grinning little faces with mischievous brown eyes – our children in the ward at present. One little fellow, Hosein of only seven years, was coming to Meshed with his mother on pilgrimage, and en route he fell off a donkey and broke his right arm. The bones were set and the arm bound up by a village bone-setter, and when he arrived in Meshed the entire hand was black with gangrene, and the whole forearm infected. Only amputation could be advised. However, he is in fact adjusting himself to the loss of his forearm, and can play his harmonica just as effectively with his left hand! Mara is a wiggly little girl with a toothless grin who is under treatment for a form of ringworm of the scalp, a very prevalent disease among children that leaves them bald, or partially so, in spots. Soghra, the daughter of a *sayid* (honoric title), and therefore superior to the rest of us, had about seven eighths of the larger bone of her right leg removed because of an extensive osteomyelitis. She alternately laughs and cries when we do her dressing, and at the sight of any new instrument fears another operation. And cute little Mohammed, how can I adequately describe his adorable smile and giggle! His father is a leper in our leper village. Mohammed developed mastoiditis and we operated on him several weeks ago. At first he was such a thin solemn little boy, then as his physical condition began to improve, he blossomed out with shy smile and now he is full of mischief, and his cheeks are rotund and rosy. And then there is little Fatimeh of 12 years, with a wizened old face, literally only skin and bones, for she weighs 30 pounds. Her blind beggar father brought her in. We hope, but we cannot promise, to send her home fat and healthy again. Probably they will insist on taking her away just as she begins to gain a bit.

The majority of our adult patients (on the women's side) are young women from 16 to 30, but they would seem older than a similar group in America. They are a loveable lot on the whole, once they have been cleaned up, and accustomed themselves to our peculiar ways – sleeping on a bed, being made to stay in bed, wearing pajamas and washing in a basin! The older women are often quite childlike and pathetic. We have such a funny old soul, now. She insisted on coming into the hospital for an operation and even paid five dollars for it. Five months ago she had been shot accidentally and a few small birdshot lodged under the skin. This spring she traveled fourteen *fareschs* (56 miles) on foot from Nishapur to have us remove them, and though we could only locate definitely one small shot the size of a 'French pea' which was doing her no harm, we could not dissuade her from her desire for an operation. You should have seen her delight and triumph when I handed over to her the piece of lead. "Ah hah, look! I knew it was there," she cried. She tied it up carefully in her scarf, for I told her it was worth five *tomans* to her. I trust she will be happy now, though we did only remove one, and is reassured that she won't die because the others may still be there. Today she showed me some grease wrapped up in a piece of newspaper, which she wanted to rub on her wound! We have great fun with her.

Now that the warm sun shines again and the air is soft and spring-like, our wards are vacated for the porch. Would that we had more porch space for the women, and especially a place for the many patients with tuberculosis in all its various forms. For Persian's sun is the best germ-killer, wound-healer, and tonic that we have! Were it not for the hot sun the country would be far worse than it is medically speaking.

SCENES ON AN AFTERNOON WALK

EDUCATIONAL BULLETIN,
ST. JOHN'S PRESBYTERIAN CHURCH

Extracts from recent letters by Dr. Adelaide Kibbe of Meshed, Persia, received in April, 1931

We all took a nice walk outside of the city. The washerwomen were out in full force (washing in the irrigation pools) – a never failing source of interest these washerwomen and their funny display of clothes, all colors, shapes and sizes and so many of them stretched along the road for a quarter of a mile. Passed the graveyard. Always a new grave being dug there and I never can see where they can find space for another. Village folk coming into town atop their creaking wooden carts piled high with full bags and possessions, donkeys loaded with brush wood, cows, mule trains, didn't see any camels today. We did stop in to see an old potter at work with his clay – making water vessels – and seven generations before him had been potters. Mr. Steiner asked him where he learned his trade. He said God taught it to him. He teaches all trades! Then he started in to philosophize and went clear back to Noah. He said he was the first potter. By this time he had shaped and patted and finished the bowl. He has probably made thousands of pieces, all by hand.

Next we investigated an icehouse. The kind shaped like a beehive with very thick walls. They freeze the water in a straight runway, chop it up and store it in these houses for summer use.

Have been doing several tonsillectomies recently. One who did not take the anesthetic very well did not come back to the clinic afterward, but sent her brother. He said that, "ever since the operation their donkey had been very sick."

MORE RESPONSIBILITY

A LETTER FROM DR. ADELAIDE KIBBE IN THE AMERICAN HOSPITAL AT MESHED, PERSIA

Dated April 22, 1932, reads in part as follows:

The weeks fly by rapidly, even in Oriental countries, and spring has firmly pushed winter aside now, and our gardens are bursting forth in all their beauty of green. Warm days have come and we are almost ready for our summer routine, though rainstorms must still come if crops are to be good this year. In some ways Persia is quite similar to California in climate.

The last two months have been especially busy, for in March Dr. Lichtwardt was in Teheran three weeks, leaving me in charge of the hospital – always quite a responsibility for my shoulders. Upon his return Miss Reynolds, our woman evangelist, and I had planned to go on a women's evangelistic and medical itinerating trip to Nishapur – an experiment for us, which we were anxious to undertake. But, as I have not yet been able to obtain my license to practice medicine in Persia (due mostly to the Persian Government's insufficient and procrastinating methods) a temporary permit was promised to enable me to do work in another city – by April first. It hasn't come yet, much to our disappointment and so, though practically all our equipment and complicated preparations as medicines, and so on, were ready – we have had to call off the trip. Word somehow got to our Nishapur friends and to villagers around about, and they were glad we were coming – and many women were anxious for the 'woman doctor' to come. Also we have a nice group there of friends, many of whom are really interested in Christianity, and a few have bravely professed their loyalty to Christ. They need encouragement and help. Unfortunately, we shall have to wait two years now, because Miss Reynolds goes on her first furlough this fall.

Perhaps it was better that we didn't go after all, for the day before our intended departure I became ill again with a mild attack of rheumatic fever, not serious but enough to keep from work for two months. I am gradually feeling more my old self again.

In Meshed there is no lack of work for us, our clinics are almost more than we can handle and the wards as full as we care to have them. This good weather brings villagers in from distant places, all means of travel are used including the popular 'autol' as the uneducated call it. And occasionally strange patients buy a ticket. Dr. Lichtwardt treated a poor, sick monkey last week – a lame back, probably tuberculosis. He also has a cow and a camel on his famous sick list! He referred the cow to me, but I didn't relish the job, much, and sent her back.

It is rather hard for us to appreciate out here the financial condition America is in. We do sympathize with our friends and know you are probably all bearing heavy burdens in one way or another that we do not realize.

I trust my letter thanking the Woman's Association and all who helped prepare the hospital report arrived last winter. Letters between here and there have a way of getting lost far too frequently. Occasionally they turn up several months late. Replies are still arriving from various parts of the world on receipt of the report. I think it has been well received and we are all ever so grateful to those in St. John's Church who had a share in it.

HOUSE CALLS

Annual Personal Report
June 1932

A doctor does undoubtedly have an opportunity to go into the houses and home life of our Persian friends that others do not have. So in retrospect of the past year I shall relate a few experiences of various house calls made, not that I am called so often, but at times it is necessary for us to go to the homes. A house call can be more or less of an adventure – where will it be in the city, what kind of a home, clean or dirty, a spacious courtyard or a cramped little place, friendly people or strict Mohammedans who will eye me with distrust, former friends or new ones to be made, and of course, will my knowledge and experience be equal to the task ahead of me? I have time enough to thus contemplate as I jog along in a *droshky*, though occasionally I am whisked to my destination in a comfortable motorcar. As a rule, one learns little from the relative or friend sent as guide, for clothes and general appearances are deceiving in this country, and the information they have to impart somehow is always insufficient and inaccurate. If it is winter time, much bundling up in coats, sweaters, scarves, mittens, galoshes, etc. is necessary for the probable long ride and late return, but in summer the joy of only a light coat, hat, my trusty handbag and a flashlight. So while our horses are trotting along over rough cobblestones, around sharp, narrow corners, in and out of traffic, avoiding by only a hair's breadth donkeys and heedless pedestrians who care little for traffic and use sidewalk and street indiscriminately, let us think a bit about the homes of Persia as a doctor sees them.

There comes before me most vividly the picture of the 'crazy girl'. One evening just at dusk I climbed into a carriage and was driven by devious route and brought to the other side of the city. We stopped before a dark, narrow passageway, which I entered trustfully. As I stepped into the court a single lamp set on the ground gave a dim light, enough so I could see that the place was a large, clean flagged courtyard surrounded on all four sides by a two-story building with an upper balcony. In the

center of the yard was a water reservoir with a wooden
cover. The whole place had an air of desolation, no green
trees or shrubs that one usually finds even around the
smallest of houses, no sound of laughter or the voices of
the inevitable neighbor. To one side, sitting on a rug, I
could see in the half-light a young girl, while an older man
was kneeling beside her holding her hands. Two or three
women in their house *chaddors* flitted around, one spread
a rug for me, another brought a lamp, and then they all
with anxious faces sat down near us. In the better light I
could see that the girl was indeed quite young, about 14,
probably Jewish, with dark curly hair and a pretty face,
though there was a restless, unnatural look in her eyes.
I learned that for several months previous she had been
acting peculiarly, then about a week ago she had been
married and following this, she suddenly had a complete
mental breakdown. Now she was 'wild', difficult to restrain
and impossible for her family to manage. Later I saw that
beneath her *chaddor* her ankles were in heavy chains with
great padlocks for double protection. They knew no other
way to restrain her, and the tragic part was what I could
do to help her. For Persia has no hospital or provision for
the mentally sick, and we simply could not accept her as
a patient. I could only give certain suggestions for caring
for her in as humane and sympathetic a way as possible.
But I felt, and saw, the despair, hopelessness and lack of
understanding in the faces of her parents, and the futility
and inadequacy of the situation.

Again it was night when I went on a call to a house
within a short distance of our compound gate. It was
during the month of *Moharram*, the month of mourning
throughout Shiah Islam over the death of Hassan and

Hosein. Every night groups of men and women gather together in different places, a home or a mosque, or a tent arranged especially for the purpose, to hear again from the *Mullah* the story of the tragedy and to work up intense feeling and grief over the wrongs done to their Imams some thousand years ago. As I approached this house I heard coming from within, the sound of the *Mullah's* voice, the chanting of the men, and the weeping and wailing of the women. There in the doorway were rows and rows of shoes in precise order, now I could see the men sitting in the center of the court, the women grouped at the rear of the gathering, the *Mullah* in long robe and white turban was reading from a big book, probably the Quran. My guide went boldly into the yard, motioned me to follow, and vanished. I was hesitant to follow, to enter such a company alone at this time; I, a *kafir* (non-Muslim), be openly seen at a *rosh khan* (prayer meeting), in *Moharram*! Then I saw a familiar face, one of our gardeners, and after he had reassured me, I entered quickly, crossed the yard and found my patient in a small room off the main court, apparently not the least disturbed by the noise without. When I returned through the yard a small group of men were standing in a circle, chests bared, and in unison they beat their chests with their hands, crying out, 'Hassan, Hosein'. I looked all I dared, and went out silently wondering just what comfort or reassurance to the spirit there could be in such a proceeding.

Another time it was early morning of a warm spring day, soft, clean air, and the sun barely showing to the east when I walked quickly to a little home not far away, a Turkish family. In the small untidy room I had to step over several sleeping children to reach the patient. There on the floor surrounded by numerous neighbors, friends and children (who, though I repeatedly shooed them out, always returned like flies to the honey jar) I delivered my first pair of twins.

I was rather annoyed one evening to be called away from a little dinner part just at the 'strawberries on ice cream' stage. After a rapid change of clothing and a long bumpy ride across the city with an anxious husband as guide, I came to a large, well-kept and attractive house, (behind its high wall, of course), with numerous servants standing around. When I entered the room I saw the woman sitting up comfortably, laughing, and rather sheepishly, she said that she had had a pain in stomach but it was all gone now! So I returned to my party, and had the satisfaction of having earned five *tomans* for the hospital anyhow, in between courses.

But for me the most difficult and unpleasant part of the work is to get those who can afford to pay to 'come across', in a slang phrase. A young policeman came to the hospital to say that his wife was in great pain and could I come at once. I explained our fee, and he said, "You see I am a policeman and you know we get less than five dollars a month. I can't possibly pay what you ask." In the end of course I went with him. He had been recently married, and his room was clean and orderly, well supplied with household necessities. In one corner, a large table was neatly arranged with the wedding gifts, mirrors, glassware and fancy boxes dear to the heart of the Persian bride. I then could see they must have more than his salary upon which to live, yet I had to accept the pittance he paid. Several weeks later in the hospital corridor a well-dressed, rather violently perfumed young man spoke to me. "You don't know me, do you? I am a policeman, and you came to see my wife one day." After that I extracted from him, with difficulty of course, a more reasonable amount for a minor operation and clinic frees. That is only one instance of what we have to contend with daily.

Occasionally I drive in state in a fine car to a beautiful home set in an extensive and well-kept garden. The spacious stone house has an imposing entrance, and within are beautiful rugs and furnishings. One bitterly cold, blowy winter day I drove in an open carriage to the mansion of the general of the army, and felt quite important with an officer as an escort perched up on the box beside the driver.

But now we have arrived at last in the older part of the city, and leave our carriage to go down the narrow street to the little door at the end. The small courtyard is filled, so it seems, with children of all ages, for evidently several live here. I am led up high, steep, outside steps to the second story, and there in a hot stuffy little room, inconceivably ill kept, have gathered the usual number of neighbors to talk and argue and suggest. The patient is a weak, long-suffering little woman, who is twenty-two years old, has been married eight years, and has had six children. They tell me they have done everything to help her, burned all manner of incense, held a pan of coals over her head, torn her *chaddor* in half, poured water through her husband's shirt and gave her the water to drink, and even shook her in a blanket, but to no avail. Contrary to the usual thing, I am able to persuade them to bring her to the hospital, her only chance, for possibly

we can help her. God knows better, and once again a
Persian mother gives her life.

Respectfully submitted
Adelaide Kibbe

Photo 3.6 Adelaide and Mabel on city wall outside Meshed

Photo 3.7 Vakilabad in the mountains above Meshed

CELEBRATING TRADITIONAL HOLIDAYS

A LETTER FROM ADELAIDE KIBBE, AT MESHED,

November 25, 1932

Today is Thanksgiving and I imagine only a few of you are up as yet, for its not quite 8:00 in California. We are all celebrated and dined and ready for reading or letters and bed. This morning our little group of eight grownups and two children gathered for a service. We sang *America* with as much pride and love as ever and had a good talk by Mark Irwin, our newest member. Then came the turkey and all the fixings (except cranberries – but we had a jelly made from a local berry that was cranberry red and not dissimilar in taste). Then came ping-pong for exercise and a walk in the crisp, cold air – outside the city wall – too cold to go very far. It seemed quite a festive occasion and we are happy that we can make the day as nearly like home as possible.

Christmas is a very busy time for us all, for we have two teas for our Persian women friends, the Persian Christian Christmas service and one for non-Christians, our English Christmas service for those outside the mission, and our own Christmas festivities and a party or two! We have not decided yet how to entertain the women – always a problem. Last year we gave *Why the Chimes Rang*, in pantomime and they loved it and still speak of it. We are watched so closely now and marvel that as much as we do carry on is permitted – so we have to be careful of what we choose – and not give it too much publicity.

I wonder what President Reinhardt said about Religion in Russia. Of course, I have never been in Russia, but we do get some of the little sideline by-plays and repercussions of what is going on amongst their own peasantry. I have remarked before on these good, stolid Russians who come to our services with such evident joy and reverence – apparently so glad to worship without fear. Just the other Sunday a woman patient – a Russian refugee, came to the morning service and afterwards with a happy smile said to several of us in broken Persian "It is so good to be in a meeting again – so very good". The Russian refugees are still pouring into Meshed – without food, clothes, or money – poor things. And we hear tales of a terrible famine in certain parts of Russia now. Some of these articles one reads, doesn't strike a genuine note to me, at least not complete information[8].

Our first snow has come and it is quite cold – so that hospital work will gradually decrease from now on. No villager wants to walk many miles through snow and mud – even for an emergency.

Emergencies either get well or die off and chronic cases continue on for four or five months longer. We have been pretty busy this fall and will rather welcome time to read during clinic hours!

I forgot to mention the success of the Afghan trip. Everything proved most interesting, all went smoothly and Dr. and Mrs. Lichwardt spent several days in Herat. Miss Reynolds and her party went on through to Kabul

---

8   Between 1930 and 1032 Stalin forced collectivization of farmland and deportation of landholders, resulting in famine in the Ukraine and Kazakhstan. During this time he also banned the importation of bibles and encouraged the destruction of churches.

and out through India. The trip is an absolutely safe one and they had recommendations all along the line, so were well entertained and well cared for. They said Kabul was a beautifully situated city and had some quite modern ways, strange to say. Of course, they were objects of much curiosity all over the country, for few foreign women make the trip.

If we could get permission or have some arrangement made whereby we work through the board for the government, there would be great opportunity for medical work – none for evangelistic or educational work direct, as yet. We have a good many Afghan patients here in Meshed, who don't forget us.

Sincerely,
Adelaide

Photo 3.8 Visiting with villagers outside Meshed

Wanted – A Hard Job

Forbid for me an easy place,

O God, in some sequestered nook

Apart to lie,

To dose and dream and weaker grow

And less and less to do or know

Until I die!

Give me, O Lord, a task so hard

That all my powers shall taxed be

To do my best;

That I may stronger grow in toil,

For harder service fitted be,

Until I rest!

This my reward – development

From what I am to what thou art.

For this I plead!

Wrought out by being wrought upon

By deeds reflexive, done in love,

For those in need!

Charles Earle

CHAPTER 4

Putting down Roots 1933—1935

COMPARISONS AND CONTRASTS

Personal Report

1932-33

Dr. Adelaide Kibbe
Meshed

This year I feel I have been here long enough to warrant the making of comparisons and contrasts between conditions as they are now, and as they were 'when I first came to Persia'. It all depends on the subject at hand how long I have been here – if it is reflections cast at the incompleteness of my knowledge of the Persian language, then it is about three years and six months, maybe nine months. But if it's a matter of what a veteran missionary I have become than I admit that it is nearly

four years. So after four whole winters and almost four
whole summers in Meshed, and having traveled around
the country from Shiraz to the Caspian Sea, I claim the
right to reminisce and comment upon the changes and
developments of the country.

STREET LIFE

A very important acquisition of the city brought to mind
these hot, dusty days, (at least I am sure the driver feels
his importance from his superior, condescending air), is
the modern, shiny red, water wagon which rolls along at
a dignified rate and shoots out its two powerful streams
of water – which, I found, stopped for no one! No more
will we see, as in the old days, the horse cart with a large
tank of water perched upon it, and projecting from the
spout at the back, a long hose which a man walking along
behind solemnly wagged from side to side and quite
effectually wet down the dust of the streets. The streets
have developed from the little narrow winding *kuches*
of old Meshed into several broad avenues, most of them
within the last four years. Down these modern streets
go many jaunty carriages carrying men, and surprising
to see, occasionally Persian women sitting beside them,
with the top of the carriage up however, according to the
law still prevailing in Meshed for all Persian women. Or, if
she prefers to walk and is quite 'advanced', man and wife
may even saunter down the avenue side by side instead
of her keeping a respectful distance in the rear. One sees
many stylishly dressed women with long skirts, and all
the accessories, including short hair or a knot at the neck
instead of long braids down the back beneath their black
chaddors. It is said quite a few Persian women go abroad

without *chaddors*, but they are no longer distinguishable from the rest of us, they have lost their unique place. And, I fear those keeping abreast with the rapid changes in Persia rather look down on the village folk and those slow to accept foreign customs – for instance: the women who still follow behind their husbands and carry the bundles; the village women who have not discarded full trousers and the white head (band) with open work inset across the eyes; or the man in long full coat but without a collar, only a turquoise stud. One should be prepared and never intimate surprise if even a beggar, a humble shopkeeper or a servant comes out with '*Merci, Madame*' for it is quite the thing to say.

Money, too, has entered into the transformation of Persia. Formerly all common coins in circulation were one, two, or five *kran* pieces. Now you may be given in change a handful of neat little paper notes of several denominations 'made in America', lighter to carry, but it seems to go faster than in the old days. Yes, there is even a style in diseases, instead of complaining of 'wind', the favorite lay diagnosis in these regions, the patient glibly asks if it isn't '*appendiceet*' that is causing the pain, when more likely it's worms or old-fashioned stomach ache from too much *pilau*. I have noticed that a few more Persian women, mostly of the educated classes, are willing to come into the hospital, where previously the majority of our hospital cases were Armenians, Russians, or Russian-influenced Turks.

The other morning I was riding down one of the avenues that leads around Meshed's famous shrine, and there in a little side street I noticed a large canvas painting resting against the side of a building, and in front of it, a camera in position to function. The painting was vivid, striking, of enormous proportions (in fact one might say it was awful), without perspective and of glaring colors. A somber brown cliff rose up in the foreground, green grass and tall trees grew on the shore at its base, and on the brilliant blue water rode a steam ship of monstrous size, headed straight for the open sea. There seemed pathos in that – certainly incongruous – it was on Meshed's dry and windy plain hundreds of miles from any body of water. A picturesque villager in the big city on business and pilgrimage (he who has probably never seen a lake, or sea, or large river in his life), in his wanderings around town finds our photographer and his dazzling landscape – irresistible it becomes in its novelty. An unnatural background for an uncouth villager, or any who live in an inland country, but of course to him it was different, novel, foreign. Somehow it suggested and illustrated the background of all of these changes in Persia. Changes just about as startling as that picture – sudden, ruthless orders to abandon that and adopt this, customs foreign to the country, bold strokes, some successful and of value, others too much so, conceived as they are from foreign ways not worthy of imitation – often effects inharmonious with oriental life. Recently, in the foreground are appearing intelligent, educated, thinking young men who in newspaper articles are fearlessly and rightly endeavoring to make the Persian public realize that all foreign customs – including yo-yos, cafes, cinemas and things more serious – are not best for Persia, urging people to retain some of their own, old, time-honored customs, far wiser and happier for modern Persians.

SCENES OF DAILY LIVING

Personal Report
1933-34

Dr. Adelaide Kibbe
Meshed

If one could look *Through Magic Casements*[9] at the year just gone by, perhaps only the unusual, the fascinating would be visible, that which would delight and interest and satisfy, for the sordid might be lost in the background, the commonplace softened by time. So do certain incidents of this year stand out.

PATIENT TYPES

Forget that which may have been harsh, unpleasant, or daily routine, and look at a few of the more interesting pictures:

- There is the 'G.P.' (grateful patient) who dashed into my dispensary one busy morning last fall, waving an open bottle of perfume in one hand, the glass stopper in the other. She approached me, all smiles and eagerness, dabbed the violent stuff all over my white gown and my face, kissed me soundly on both cheeks, and I gravely, in return, kissed her. Then, both hands outstretched, she presented me with a silk handkerchief by which to remember her. She was sincere in her appreciation of what we were able to do for her, which always gives one a pleasant glow of satisfaction in this rather difficult business of healing the sick.

---

9   Adelaide is most likely referring to Lillian Eaton's book *Through Magic Casements: 12 stories for home and kindergarten, 1923*.

- A tragic picture is the chubby body of a little boy brought into us a few minutes after he had been found drowned in the open pool of the courtyard, unfortunately so necessary in a city where plumbing is unknown. After prolonged and tiring work we had to tell the father nothing we could do was of any avail.

- Can you see the mischief in little Hajar's bright brown eyes as she tried to work an old trick on her nurses? I heard she offered them her two precious gold bracelets if they would let her alone and not do her dressings daily, always a tearful process.

- And, sturdy six-year-old Hassan, picked up in the street with a broken leg, was a scared, pitiful child when carried into the hospital that night. However, he proved a most cheerful little patient, singing, laughing and playing with his beloved green and yellow oilcloth turtle throughout his six weeks stay.

- Then, alone and to one side, is Khadifeh, a leper woman, unlovely, deformed, illiterate but not without a sense of the eternal for she said to Miss Reynolds after the weekly Bible lesson, "Oh I know all about this world and the world to come, too, only I can't tell or express what I know."

OPIUM

In the spring of the year an opium poppy field is a lovely sight, thousands of white blossoms against the blue sky and distant green hills, but one never fails to think of the misery and sickness of body and mind that comes from these beautiful flowers! Every so often an emergency call comes to us and we rush over to administer treatment to someone who has taken, deliberately, an overdose of opium, generally, a poor foolish woman, who after a quarrel with her husband has resorted to an ancient method of regaining his favor. We usually can bring her around to a normal state, and with a few well-chosen words of advice, sending her home on her husband's arm.

FLOWERS

Glance with me through the casement at the magic of the change of seasons in our own quiet gardens. The riot of color of the gay zinnias, asters and chrysanthemums suddenly becomes the somberness of late fall, and then the cold beauty of mid-winter's dazzling white garment over every bush and trees is followed just as surely by the beautiful blossoms of pear tree, sweet scented violets, iris, and dainty columbine. Another pleasure from our garden is sharing the flowers with others, especially the sick in the hospital. In the early spring at the Persian New Years' time we pick big trays full of fragrant violets, enough to put a bunch into each patient's hand, for they love flowers. Scarlet poppies, blue bachelor's buttons and red tulip grow wild in the wheat fields in great profusion. But a true Persian likes best a small pink rose to dangle in his hand.

During the year I have gone to Teheran, not for rest alone, but also for business in the capital city; spent a week or two in the mountains playing and resting; taken a most interesting ten day donkey trip into the high mountains, and always I am content to return to home and garden and work.

Respectfully submitted,
Adelaide Kibbe

Photo 4.1 Upper row: Dr. Lichtwardt, Lisle Steiner, Dr. M. Donaldson. Next row: (Mark) Irwin with baby, Hilda Lichtwardt, Elizabeth Reynolds, Mabel Nelson, Dr. Adelaide Kibbe. Lower: Mrs. Irwin, Marion Lichtwardt, Lois Steiner, Chas. Edw. Steiner, Bess Donaldson Bottom row: Bobby Steiner, Harlow Lichtwardt, Billy Steiner

STREET SCENES

Watercolors in possession of author. Originally purchased by Adelaide Kibbe during her years in Iran

Photo 4.2 Soup Seller
E. Savachian, Teheran, 1957

Photo 4.3 Mullah
Demon, Teheran, 1931

Photo 4.4 Hamal
E. Savachian, Teheran, 1957

Photo 4.5 Street Barber
K.Peshapour, 1935

Visit our Hospital for a Weekend
Adelaide Kibbe, M.D.

Presbyterian Mission, Meshed, Persia

Does a weekend at the Meshed hospital appeal to you, not as a 'ticket patient', but rather as an interested visitor? You may have your choice of summer or winter and if you choose the former a sun helmet is necessary, and a tennis racquet for off hours, and if the latter, a fur coat and galoshes. Should you accept our invitation you will not be able to breakfast in bed at nine o'clock for hospital prayers begin at seven-thirty in summer and eight o'clock in winter. Everyone attends and one would be conspicuous by one's absence.

So we shall pretend that you have come, more preferably in early summer when one can enjoy the cool freshness of early morning – Friday morning in fact. This week some of the literate Persian helpers are leading prayers, all having gathered at the booming of the big camel bell in the hall, the men assistants, the male nurses, the cook and his two boy helpers, doorkeepers, and the engine man, or women nurses in simple blue *chaddors*, washerwomen and cleaners. We generally sing a hymn together, have a scripture reading, short talk and prayer, and then we are ready for the day's adventure. And, each day is an adventure, for invariably something new and unexpected happens. Our helpers are not all Christians, but all are willing to come to our daily prayer service.

WARD ROUNDS

Women first, though in Moslem countries it is so often otherwise, so we will go upstairs and make rounds on the women's side and then in the men's wards. If you happen to be a gentleman, just try to look wise at medical terms and be nonchalant at the sight of bloody wounds, and the women will probably think you are a doctor and not object to our tour of inspection. We have now about twenty beds for our women patients. These are divided into three wards, light and cheerful with the morning sun. We put all the patients that we can out on the porch for sun treatment, and wish the porch were larger, for the sun is Persia's best therapeutic agent and germ-killer. Perhaps several bright, brown-eyed little children will greet you with a *salaam* and a giggle, or there may be only old wrinkled women with kindly smiles, and younger women, really only girls, with the tired look of poverty and much child-bearing. Occasionally a light-haired, stolid Russian or German is the silent occupant of a bed, unable to talk to the other women who would like to be friendly. Usually there is a baby or two who can't be separated from the source of its daily food supply, asleep in a hammock under the next bed so that its mother can better swing it with a string! We feed all of our patients unless they desire to bring special food from home, and visitors are only allowed afternoons, though at times one does slip through out of hours. This is not the rule in most Mission hospitals, but in Meshed the Persian city hospital is even more strict than we are, so we feel that we can demand this. Certainly, it is easier for both patient and nurse for seldom is it 'a' visitor but often all of their relatives, neighbors and children who come.

TWENTY BEDS IN MEN'S WARDS

Now down the broad corridor, past the operating suite, and turn to the left. Here we enter the men's wards with their twenty beds. As the days and nights are warm now the beds are all out on the big porch. Lucky men! We walk down past them – young bearded men, old bearded men, grandpas with wrinkled-up eyes and toothless grins, often with bushy, fiery red whiskers, again the evidence of the vanity of men, and the abundance of henna! Many of them are only too glad of a home and food, and though they may have been filthy dirty on admission, they seem to enjoy a bed with sheets and being fed. 'You know how men are!' We have attempted to standardize our inpatient records this year by preparing special printed forms for the history and the physical examination which can be more rapidly and efficiently filled out and filed away.

PRIVATE ROOMS

The private rooms, seven of them, open off the men's corridor, and are available for either men or women as needed. There is always a great fluctuation in their occupancy. Sometimes all may be occupied, again for a short period all may be vacant. Wealthy Afghans frequently demand the 25 *toman* a week rooms. Our private rooms are a source of good revenue for the hospital. The amount paid more than covers the expenses, and allows us to take care of a certain number of indigent patients. (A *toman* equals a dollar, although present exchange has lowered its value.)

CLINIC DAY

Today is clinic day. The patients for an hour or more have been gathering downstairs on the porch, in the waiting rooms for men and women, and all over the yard with their donkeys, carts, camels, and even an auto or two. The doorkeepers sell their tickets trying to decide who can justly pay two *krans* and who should pay more. We disappear into the doctors' rooms and prepare for three or more hours of real work. Dr. Lichtwardt usually goes into the waiting room, reads a few verses from the Bible and makes a short prayer before we start seeing patients. If you would like to go out into the porch and enter the door at the end, you will usually find Miss Elizabeth M. Reynolds, the evangelistic worker for women, talking to the women, showing them pictures and reading Bible stories to them, making a happy use of the time while they are waiting to see the doctor.

HOUSE CALLS

House calls may come at any time of the day or night, and fussy patients and relatives are found in Persia as well as in America. On account of the fact that there are a certain number of European trained doctors in Meshed who can aid in giving treatment to the people of the city, it is not our policy to make many medical visits in the homes. We are, however, called out frequently in consultation with the Persian doctor, and try to do as much of this work as possible in late afternoon so as not to interfere with the regular routine of the hospital. Of course babies wait for no one.

MESHED, A PILGRIMAGE CENTER

Because Meshed is a city of pilgrims we have all types coming. They are not only our own city folk, but travelers, Kurdish men and women, the women in long full skirts of red, leather slippers of green and gold, and head dress of black. Afghans, tall dark men in white baggy trousers and great white turbans, do not often bring their women. Baluchis come with their women decked out in interesting gold and silver jewelry. Simple village folk, hulking men in funny 'bowl' haircuts, and women in coarse *chaddors*, have had to ride several days on camels or donkeys, or have even come on foot to Meshed. Most of them are pilgrims coming from all over Persia to the shrine of the Holy City.

OPERATIONS ON SATURDAYS

It is Saturday morning now, prayers are over, rounds are made, and our operating schedule for today is arranged. The great *samovar* is steaming away (the source of hot water for the operating rooms), and possibly the two larger rooms and the smaller room too will be in use. An average morning's work might include two cataracts, one on a wealthy Persian who is paying 50 *tomans* for his operation, another one on an old man from a village, his left eye entirely gone, his other eye to be operated on today in the hope of saving enough vision to keep him from becoming a beggar on the streets; an iridectomy on the eye of a little child almost blind from trachoma; the removal of a bladder stone from a little Afghan boy, attended by his devoted and anxious father; tuberculous glands cleaned up, and several entropions for the assistants to take care of. Formerly, patients' relatives were allowed in the operating rooms, and we have not been able to do away with it entirely, but we are trying to persuade them of the wisdom of remaining outside. This they will do as they gradually gain confidence in foreign doctors. If anything is taken out of a patient, the patient and his relatives are always eager to see it and even keep it – anything from teeth, bladder stones, and hernia sacs to glands, appendices and tonsils! Something tangible which you can show them always impresses them with the necessity and value of the operation.

THE LEPER VILLAGE

Saturday afternoon is leper day and you can ride out with Dr. Lichtwardt weekly with several dressers, the druggist, and also Miss Reynolds. He goes out two miles to the leper village by *droshky* to give them their injections, treatments and necessary medicines. Miss Reynolds reads and talks to the leper women, and has been teaching them knitting. The work this year with the lepers has continued on steadily as in previous years, but we have found that the biweekly visits to the leper village were not essential as this gave them too intensive treatment. So now we are going but once a week as in the first few years. Progress is slow but there are signs of definite improvement in many, and actual cure in a few. We are rather disappointed in the lack of increasing cooperation by the Persian government in this work, as we feel they ought to take a more active part in what is distinctly a health problem of Persia.

THE SUNDAY SERVICE

A peaceful Sunday morning it is with a little more leisure for doctor and nurse. This makes the day different and more restful, though one can never tell what the day may bring forth. For instance there was a run of obstetrical cases for three or four Sundays. By nine-thirty all ambulatory hospital patients and little children in casts are taken down stairs for the morning evangelistic service, the men up in front, the women sitting in back. This service is always attended by outside folk as well. The little children of the hospital love to go and consider it the treat of the week. They listen pretty well, though when some old man up front heaves a tremendous sigh in the middle of the prayer or sermon it causes evident mirth. In winter someone has always to be on guard to see that a newcomer does not sit on the hot stove in his confusion upon entering such a congregation of people who perch up on chairs and benches instead of comfortably sitting on the floor. Patients come in thinking it is clinic morning. They are given a seat and treated to a good evangelistic talk before they are told there is no clinic this morning, but unless it is an emergency, they must come back early the next day. Babies cry and talk aloud; little children run around and grin shyly up at you; late comers wander in, *salaam* in a clear voice, and always seem to have difficulty finding a seat, so that one or two of the audience inevitably rise up to help them; donkeys bray outside impatient of their master's delay; someone talks aloud to his neighbor asking what it is all about; a patient is overcome by a coughing fit and has to leave – but the preacher must preach on despite such distraction! After the service there are always many to *salaam* and shake hands with (one of our customs which they overwork), then the nurses pilot their charges back to bed and the children are carried up stairs. Your weekend visit is over.

In our daily morning devotions together, prayer is always made that the sick coming to our hospital may be healed both in body and in mind. And, we who are responsible for the hospital and its influence feel that this expresses our desire also:

'But some have more sin than fever

And some have more grief than pain

God help me make whole both body and soul

Before they go out again'

Anonymous

(Location of original publication not identified. Possibly a church newsletter or magazine.)

PERSONAL AND SOCIAL EVENTS

RANDOM ABSTRACTS FROM RECENT LETTERS
OF DR. ADELAIDE KIBBE, MESHED PERSIA

ST. JOHN'S PRESBYTERIAN CHURCH, BERKELEY,
CALIFORNIA, NEWSLETTER 1934

Helen Hoffman (Mrs. Dr. Hoffman) has been getting up
a big Russian Christmas party and tree for the Russian
Refugees today (Russian Christmas Jan 13). Her big,
generous heart takes her into all manner of work. Instead
of any useless presents, all worthy (and only the worthy
and deserving are invited), are to be given clothing, dress
goods, comforters and blankets, mattresses, and so on,
for they are living (in) this cold, snowy weather with just
next to nothing.

LICE

You would certainly laugh if you could have seen me
having my head searched this afternoon 'Going Hunting'
as we say in Persian. Yes, I mean for lice! We have had a
sudden incentive to have our heads inspected, for I found
Mrs. Irwin's head just full of 'em! Where she ever got them
remains a mystery, but her hair and clothes were full of
them! So we are looking. We who work with the clinic
patients have plenty of opportunity, surely, to pick them
up. I frequently find them on my outside gown, but never
in my clothes or hair yet. Fleas, yes. But they say, "You
aren't a real Musselman unless you have lice," and verily,
I believe it is so.

BURYING THE DEAD

Miss Reynolds was telling us a wild tale she heard last night. You know in this enlightened land of Persia, they carry the dead through the streets in an open, poorly made, light wood coffin – and because they don't do any embalming, just wash the body, I believe, they always bury at once. Funeral processions are frequent and the box is carried on the shoulders – any old angle, which is quite horrifying to us! Many run up from the street crowds to carry the coffin a short distance and gain *savab* (merit) in the next world. The coffin is covered with a piece of cloth – the higher the rank and station in life of the deceased the better the cloth and the more mourners and followers there are. Well, such a funeral procession was going through the bazaar last week, so they say, and a policeman stopped them to get the burial permit. They said they would get it at the 'wash house'. But the policeman insisted and finally pulled off the cover, revealing, not a dead body, but stolen goods – silver ware, *samovars* and so on! The thieves dropped the coffin and ran. Every city has its tales to tell.

HOSPITAL WORK

The hospital work is not decreasing yet, though there will be a slump around Persian New Years – then our really busy days begin! However, all beds in the ward are occupied right now. Wednesday I had an obstetrical case – little twin boys – but one died last night. Only weighed three pounds and three ounces and we have no incubator. Twins seem to be popular this year in Persia.

That same evening a little boy was brought into the hospital by one of your church elders. He had found him in the street, lying 'in the gutter' so to speak, (Persian streets have no gutters) with a broken leg, only four or five years old and apparently all alone. He said his mother was dead and his father, for some reason we couldn't make out, had left him and gone back to the village. He had fallen in a ditch and broken his leg and spent the night in the street, so we understand. Such a sad tale, all the nurses and patients were weeping while we bound his leg up in a splint. No word yet from his father.

AN INVITATION

Maybe we weren't set up this week to receive a handsome invitation from Oyster Bay to the wedding of Theodore Roosevelt Jr.'s eldest daughter to a Mr. McMillan – one of the young men who was traveling with their party across Asia last fall and was here with them. The invitation even included breakfast at Sagemore Hill after the church ceremony! They were safe, however, in sending us invitations! Still, it was most kind of them to do that and we were quite thrilled to have them.

'*NO RUZ*' CELEBRATION

Well, *No Ruz* (New Years, March 21st) calling is in the offing and we will soon be making out lists of calls for those busy afternoons from the 21st of March for ten or twelve days. Nothing else is accomplished those days, you can imagine, for we make four, six, eight calls, more or less, a day and consume much tea and nuts, but try to cut down on other sweets.

SHAH'S BIRTHDAY CELEBRATION

The Shah's birthday was yesterday and the whole city celebrated the <u>day before</u>, the <u>day itself</u> and <u>today</u>! Wednesday evening, the eve of the holiday, we were all invited to the Governor's mansion to a big shindig – evening affair. The streets were crowded with revelers – every little shop or big store had rugs hung out in front, lamps and candles or electric lights (really quite dim – the lamps make much more of a show) aglow. Tea was being served, dancers in costume, *droshkys* all decorated up with flags, paper flowers, and garlands, trucks filled (with) musicians – a gay town it was. But strange to say, the street reveling quiets down by 8:30 or 9:00 and when we went home from the party at 9:15 the streets were dark and deserted – comparatively.

In front of the governor's house it was beautifully decorated – with lines of crystal candlesticks, each on a high pedestal, with I should say 30 or 40 candles on each, lead up to the gate. Above the gate, a crown in electric lights and Persian words spelled out in lights 'Greeting to the King'. There was quite a mob around the gate but way was made for us and we went into the big, first inner court, where crowds had also gathered, perhaps fewer, only a few women in evening dress. We thought it was just for tea and left our hats and coats on. Tea was served first, of course, and general conversation. Then out in the court around the large lagoon they shot off beautiful fireworks, as pretty as any I have seen for a long time. An orchestra from the army played Persian music, not half bad, the best I've heard yet, I think. Then, just as were beginning to think of leaving, we were invited into another room where there was a long table loaded with many kinds of cold dishes – turkey white meat, chicken with fancy green sauce, salads, patties, pâté de foie gras and plenty of *wine and vodka*! Surprising for a Mohammedan crowd, but it is getting all too popular among them. All the big men of the city were there – many of whom I don't know yet – not a bad looking crowd on the whole, the general of the army and higher officers, judges, doctors, heads of the various departments in the Shrine, and so on.

Doctor Hoffman and I had to leave early as we had a big emergency operation on. It was successful, I'm very glad to say. It took so much persuading and talking on our part to get them to consent finally to an operation, so in that case I'm always especially anxious for the patient to get along all right. If they don't, I always wish we hadn't persuaded them to let us operate, even though it was the only hope.

BUILDING CONSTRUCTION METHODS

SOME MESHED HOSPITAL HAPPENINGS

RAISING THE ROOF

We might call these last few months B-D-A – before-during-after the new tin roof on the women's wing of our hospital. We planned to take off the old mud roof this fall, and knew it would be noisy and confusing, but did not expect the extensive repair that had to be done. The operating suite, men's wards and private rooms were all whitewashed and cleaned, storerooms emptied and supplies put in order, with work going in its regular routine. Dr. Kibbe and I had taken our vacation, camping up in the hills with the Steiners and returned refreshed for another year's work, when one afternoon we were called over to find the X-ray room ceiling had fallen in, and my storeroom next to it just ready to, the workmen had taken off some of the mud roof, found the beams decayed on the ends, and the smaller pieces of wood holding the mud-straw all gone.

Persian roof construction is interesting. Looking up from inside a room there is the whitewashed plaster covering, the small pieces of wood (thicker than our laths) nailed to heavy crossbeams. On top of the beams more short pieces of wood, a layer of matting or reeds, then a foot or more layer of mud mixed with straw (put on wet, allowed to dry, then rolled frequently to prevent rains from seeping through the cracks.) So when such a roof starts falling in it causes trouble. We had hoped that the beams were still good and would not need to be replaced.

So we quickly removed the X-ray apparatus, fortunately the tube was not injured, and took all the supplies we could out of my storeroom. Boxes had just arrived from Iowa women who sew for us, and my shelves were full of gowns, pajamas, bathrobes, sheets, pillowcases, sponges, operating supplies, towels, and bandages for the next year. We piled them in our small operating room, woolen blankets still in mothballs on the bottom, then comforters, pillows, and all the rest.

Next morning between operations we all worked to take our women patients over to the end of the men's wing, using an L shaped ward, two private rooms, and the porch at the end which holds ten beds. An awning protected them somewhat from the men patients and visitors who had to use the corridor. So for nearly two months the girl nurses had to work in much confusion, the first few days we nearly smothered from the dust and dirt, and noise of pounding and shouting workmen was very trying to patients and helpers. The nurses worked hard and tried to keep things in order, wails were also heard from the kitchen and laundry. "How can we cook and wash in all this dirt," but they managed.

Elizabeth Reynolds

TIME OFF

LETTER FROM ADELAIDE KIBBE, M.D. MESHED, IRAN

Last month I was alone in the hospital, save for two or three hours a day when I had help from an English doctor in town. It is always a very difficult time for one; the responsibility and extra work weigh me down! But I lived through it and find each time I do it I have gained a little in self-confidence and poise, especially in undertaking more difficult operations alone.

VACATION

Elizabeth Reynolds and I have had two grand vacations this year. A month is our privilege and we have taken it in two doses – two weeks in June when the flowers were still lovely and grass and trees a fresh green, and two weeks in August, though this year we were in the city for July's heat, and hot it was for weeks. Our first trip was as usual by donkey-back into the high mountains, this time on the very backbone of our mountains. For 10 days we were 9,000 to 11,000 feet up. First we spent three days in Deezbod – the friendly and interesting village in which Miss Reynolds is particularly interested. Being Iswailis, they are more friendly to Christians and much closer in thought and practice than are the straight Shiah Moslems. They consider the Agha Khan of India Christ's representative on earth. Miss Reynolds has made fast and loyal friends with most of the villagers; 36 have made profession of faith. Of course work had been done there before she first went there, but her influence on these folk has been considerable.

We pitched our tent on a sloping and rocky hillside (there isn't a level spot in the lovely valley – houses are one above another) and for two days I held a saddlebag clinic – rather enjoying it though realizing how very primitive it all was. They entertained us for tea and for dinner in their homes and were very friendly. The Sunday evening – our last – we had a sing for those who cared to come to our tent and a goodly crowd did. Then the next day we went up into the high mountains which was not perhaps a rest, but certainly interesting and a change. This time we have camped in one spot, another pretty valley, and been lazy – real lazy.

Photo 4.6 Swimming party on vacation camping trip

Photo 4.7 Helen Hoffman in camp

Photo 4.8 Adelaide and Meshed friends

Photo 4.9 Trek in high mountains above Meshed

As the marsh-hen secretly builds on the watery sod,

Behold I will build me a nest on the greatness of God:

I will fly in the greatness of God as the marsh-hen flies

In the freedom that fills all the space twixt the marsh

and the skies:

By so many roots as the marsh-grass send in the sod

I will lay me a-hold on the greatness of God...

Extract from The Marshes of Glynn, Sidney Lanier

CHAPTER 5

Two Homes 1936—1940

Adelaide continued her work in Meshed until 1935 when she went home for a year's furlough. Part of the process of going on furlough was to have the individual's work evaluated by fellow missionaries in a pre-furlough questionnaire. One of the considerations was whether the individual should return to the mission field:

"Has always shown readiness to adjust herself to personal preferences of others without resentment or ill will."

"Is very normal and has very best qualifications for missionary work."

"Is lacking in self-confidence and hesitates to take responsibility on that account, but has more ability than she shows."

"A thoroughly devoted, consecrated, earnest worker of moderate natural ability, an exceedingly agreeable associate to work with, always inclined to give others the benefit of the doubt."

"Very fit for missionary service." "Excellent." "Very capable."

"Has had the hospital to run alone several times."

"Has been doing very effective service and has developed from year to year."

"Have heard her very highly spoken of by nurses in the hospital."

In answer to the question where she should be assigned on return from furlough the suggestions included:

"Present work, though one thinks experience in another hospital would be valuable."

"Wherever greatest opportunity for work among women."

During a missionary's furlough they were expected to visit supporting churches and mission groups, reporting on the mission work accomplished and raising awareness of the needs of the mission field.

Photo 5.1 Visiting family while on furlough

Photo 5.2 Traveling back to Iran in 1936

Her report in 1937 reveals her feelings about returning to mission work and the changes both in Iran and where she is to be stationed next.

RETURNING TO NEW CHALLENGES

Personal Report
1937

A full year has gone by since I returned to my Meshed home with Miss Reynolds, happy to be back again, happy for work to do and for the strength to do it. The year at home was a great joy; to renew friendships, to be again with one's family, with school and church associates was indeed worthwhile. Breaking away was doubly hard this time, and would be almost impossible were it not for the compelling desire to be at work again, Christ's work, amongst Iranian friends.

I told American friends just before sailing that I was returning to a land where complete and spectacular change had taken place, the women appearing in public in foreign dress, and that I would find life quite different in Iran. As I sit at my desk during busy clinic hours and see the women of all ranks come through the door, I am amazed at the change and at their ability to adjust themselves to it. And with these changes in outward appearance has come a new desire to read, to get out into business, especially for the younger more enterprising girls. More women ask for a book to read, or pamphlets at hand, perhaps on the love of God. I do not as yet consider that our work is over here in Meshed. Most patients seem to appreciate sincerely whatever help we can give them. Certainly our full clinics and busy operating schedules throughout the year testify to the service that we can still render.

As I said at first, I feel at home in Meshed, and am exceedingly sorry to have to leave my friends and work here. If I must go to Resht perhaps a fresh start in new surroundings under new conditions will prove an unexpected blessing. As my pastor wrote me recently, 'all things work together for good to them that love God'. Two holiday excursions were donkey trips into the mountains and villages not far from Meshed. In one village, Deesbad, I held 'saddlebag' clinics for two days, seated on a little rug on the grassy slope of a small ravine. I gave out quantities of eye medicine, worm pills, and free advice, wrote numerous notes to be taken to the hospital in the city, and even cleansed a few wounds. It gives some satisfaction to know that there is work for us here, and that a woman doctor is needed too. I am constantly aware that more could be accomplished than is done. One surely needs an inexhaustible supply of a sense of humor, patience and sympathetic love.

HATS AS SYMBOLS OF CHANGE

LETTER FROM DR. ADELAIDE KIBBE OF MESHED, IRAN FOR 30TH ANNIVERSARY, SEPTEMPBER 2, 1937

Dear Friends in Saint John's:

"One Hundred years on this year", "May the year be blessed" are the good wishes from Iran for this birthday of the church. Twenty-three of these thirty years I have been a member of Saint John's Church and Sunday School. Would that I, too, could join the church family entering this evening to gather around the tables in celebration of the 30th Birthday. A happy occasion for all.

It is only a little over a year since I returned to Iran, and yet it seems longer to me, College Avenue at Derby a long distance away in actuality, but close in thought tonight. It was strange that I should have come back to Iran with quite a supply of new hats – thinking in my ignorance that I would be well stocked up for the future in a land where hats were scarce and the kind your great aunt would not wear if one were found. But I was far behind the times for if there is one thing to be found on all heads this year, it is new hats – very large white straws this summer or little toques, or berets at a rakish angle, or for some anything to cover the head. Fedoras, panamas or ordinary straws abound these hot days for the men. But I am more interested in the women who come into my clinic – hat at the proper angle, gloves and bag, and so on – amazing how they can adapt themselves to foreign dress and freedom after a lifetime of *chaddor* and seclusion. Some women naturally find adjustment difficult. They may immediately take off their hats upon entering the room – a few even leave them on when they lie down. The village women, perhaps wearing a rough felt fedora like her husband's (that might solve the new hat problem) or a modish hat from the bazaar, along with her full village skirts and nose button of turquoise, will usually park her hat any place available – stove, screen, floor or my desk – glad to have the cumbersome thing off her head. No, I did not need to bring out hats. They are to be found, though you may see your choice repeated several times in one block.

I find what I did need to bring out was a good supply of patience, patience with those who do not understand yet preventive medicine and the way to good health, those who cannot break away from the old systems of 'hot and cold', the neighborhood midwife, superstitions, and fetishes. Even though they may wear stylish hats and gay jackets, go promenading in the park, and speak glibly of their 'appendix and tonsils', there is still woeful ignorance and neglect, though the demand for modern medicine is decidedly encouraging and a stimulus to the profession. As an American I needed to bring along humility this year, for we have been *persona non grata* – though with the granting of new oil concessions this year to Americans, things are brighter. And, of course, I included an inexhaustible sense of humor, for without it one sinks into a state of faultfinding and weariness all too easily. These are only a few of supplies one should have on hand. Real love and compassion for these folk have not been mentioned and these are most important, would one work in the Name of Christ the Physician.

A number of you spoke of an indefinite hope of traveling someday. Perhaps that hope can welcome any Saint John's folk as guests; to show you our work and our city would be a keen pleasure. And I certainly owe my Saint John's friends much in thanks for the love and friendliness shown to me while in America.

Again, may the New Year be blessed for Saint John's Church.

LIFE IN RESHT

(The following was written about 1937 after her move to Resht. Recipient not identified)

If you will look in your atlas and find Iran and then the city of Resht down on the Caspian Sea, you will realize that we are off the high plateau of central Iran and down some 90 feet below sea level. Here on the coast of the Caspian the climate is damp and humid, with jungle growth and a heavy rainfall three seasons of the year. Consequently life is different here from the 'high and dry' atmosphere where I have lived for eight years. One finds different architecture in thatched roofs, red tiles and bricks instead of adobe; a different and difficult dialect of Persian; wells and damp walls that grow maiden hair ferns the envy of any florist; mildewed leather and books and verdigris on silver and brass. One hears wooden sandals clattering along the cobblestone streets (we have some newly paved avenues, too, where the elite walk in the latest models), worn, I suppose, to raise one up out of the wet and mud. Rice growing is a picturesque industry, and rice the main article of diet. In the spring and summer the women especially are seen in the fields, bending over ankle deep in muddy water, planting, weeding and caring for the tender green shoots.

You do not need much equipment to spot the child or older person with hookworm infestation, and needless to say there is much malaria, amoebiasis, sporadic typhoid and typhus fever. In connection with public health and sanitation, I have wished since reading *An American Doctor's Odyssey*[10] that this book might be translated into Persian as an inspiration for all public health officials of what might be accomplished. We have quite a number of abnormal obstetrical cases from the villages, difficult ones, and we are glad to be able to try sulfanilamide. There are several (villages) in the nearby mountain districts where leprosy is found. Often the neighbors recognize the disease fairly early and the poor unfortunate is expelled from the village. Though many are sent to the leper colony in Meshed, we still treat a number in our dispensary. Trachoma, and its complications, is far less common down here than on the plateau.

---

10   Heiser, Victor George; *An American Doctor's Odyssey: Adventures in 45 Countries*; W.W. Norton & Co., 1936.

I have mentioned only a few of the many diseases that one is called upon to diagnose and treat on a busy clinic day. Surgery comes regularly three days a week, irregularly anytime, and very nearly runs the gamut of varieties, though there are some things that we hesitate to attempt, wisely or unwisely.

Mission Report
1937-1938

This past year has brought decided changes and upheavals in my life, yet how quickly one can again settle down into a routine despite new surroundings and new customs. It was not easy last fall to pack up my belongings and say goodbye to Meshed where I had spent eight busy and happy years. Perhaps it was time to move on to different fields, and a change is often of special benefit to one making the break. Even as I am a Meshedi so someday I may become a Reshti. I have certainly appreciated the kindness and consideration of my Resht friends in making me feel at home. Though I have had a taste of three Resht seasons my spirit is not at all dampened or daunted by Resht's famous climate.

As well as becoming used to green fields, dampness, maiden hair ferns, thatched roofs and the Gilaki tongue, all of which makes Gilan seem like a different country, there are new diseases and new hospital routines with which to become acquainted. Of course many of the hospital clientele are not so sure about trusting a new doctor, and a lady doctor at that, so there have been difficulties there. Since Doctor Frame's illness people are forced to accept the woman doctor or go elsewhere. I have been kept fairly busy.

"No, we didn't bring our little boy in sooner because we thought that the tumor of his neck might get smaller of itself. Instead the tumor has become larger and our boy seems to have got smaller."

Of course, I was amused at this, but thought how often we let the lesser things, the petty worries and annoyances of our busy lives, assume such exaggerated proportions at the expense of more important matters and of our own mental equilibrium. I am still hoping someday to really learn to operate on these irritating worries and disappointments, and completely and cleanly cut them out. My mind is full of surgery these days as well as the difficulties and problems of bringing babies into the world safely, of helping diabetics on their diet, of helping malnourished infants gain weight, of patients to be freed of hookworm or amoeba, and so on.

Everyone finds it hard to be a stranger in a strange city, some more than others. One thing I miss here is more intimate and leisurely contact with Persian friends, for I am still a bit of a newcomer. This I hope to gradually accomplish as I make new friends in my work, social life and amongst the church group.

Respectfully submitted,
Adelaide Kibbe

In 1939 Adelaide spent five months back in Meshed filling in while other doctors were on furlough. A letter home to her parents gives a detailed description of a trip to a village for a local wedding.

A VILLAGE WEDDING

Hosemabad
(near Meshed)
December 8, 1939

Dear Father and Mother,

As we are waiting for a car of some kind to take us back to Meshed, I thought I might use the time in a letter to you telling of our trip to the village wedding. I have no pen along – so pencil it must be. It has been a wonderfully interesting experience, and my estimation of the villagers has risen 'way up'. They are so much more sincere, and really friendly, and very hospitable – especially kind to us. We saw and did things that I'm sure many others of our colleagues have never done. We lived with them intimately for six days, and entered into their life and celebrations as one of them, and they loved it – so did we. Elizabeth sends her love to you and says she is so thrilled we could have this last trip together. I am writing, Mother, on a small box of *Rahat Khulym* or Turkish delight flavored with cardamom and pistachio nuts. Wish you could have some. Over our knees is a big, warm sheepskin rug. Elizabeth is knitting.

TRAVELING TO THE VILLAGE

A week ago today, Friday, we packed up a few necessary things – as few as possible – our bedding rolls, the organ in a canvas cover in case of rain, three *pusteins* (sheepskin coats), the gramophone, two or three rugs, a basket of food extras (tin of sardines and beans, butter, fresh bread, pickles, fruit, candy). So Elizabeth, Gholam and I piled into a bus and rode the three hours to this stop. Here we spent the night and early in the morning started out on donkeys the eight miles up into the foothills to this village. The sun was out at times, the air crisp, distant mountains covered with snow – a fine day for a ride. We were bundled up in two layers of sweaters, old coats with fur collars, wool scarves, berets, gloves, two pairs of socks, etc., etc. We arrived about noon, and the village women folk came running out to meet us. They all know and love Elizabeth. I know a few of them – some have been patients. We found our room was to be opposite the house of the bridegroom – his brother's house, vacated for us! It was clean, a little dark, and no furniture of course, except rugs and mats on the floor, large curtains (woven by the women) at doors and windows, and a beautiful blue Indian cashmere shawl trimmed with red embroidery. Here we stayed the six days and quite comfortable, except for our poor knees which are actually swollen from sitting on the floor, which is so awkward and difficult for us.

FIRST DAY

The first afternoon and evening we were receiving friends and guests and visiting them. That night a few gathered in our room for hymn singing, which they love to do – many singing quite well. These village friends of ours are educated, not illiterate on the whole by any means – even some of the women read well. They crowded into our room, even sitting in the wall niches whenever the organ was heard. If they weren't singing, they were playing the gramophone. We had a laughing

record which they were crazy about and played so often
it was difficult for me to laugh. Mostly the records were
Persian, of course.

WEDDING PREPARATIONS

That night the bride and groom were taken to the
bath and clothes changed, and so on. The next day,
our second, the guests began coming in from distant
villages – some 75 or 100. Needless to say, it was a 'big
blowout', and our hosts not without substance and land
rather than cash. We called on the bride in her father's
house. She cried to be leaving them, and kept herself
covered with her *chaddor* (part of the ceremony). In the
afternoon we accompanied the bride to the bath where
she again changed clothes – especially interesting
wedding garments. This was a ceremony we had never
seen before – we all walked down to the bath – helping
to guide the bride who was completely veiled. Before
us went a drum and special horn which sounded like
bagpipes without the bag, and the groom's mother
danced before her. The groom was first escorted to the
bath by his friends. In the early evening friends dropped
in to talk. After supper (they insisted on feeding us –
even deputized one of the young men of the village to
wait on us – he is still with us here) we put on warm
things for it was cold, and went out to one of the nearby
rooftops where the men had gathered. A big bonfire
had been lighted, and by this light they danced, had a
funny man ride in on a donkey and do some antics. Their
dancing is most interesting – that night it was done by
two couples using large sticks which they hit together
in an intricate and difficult way as they whirled and

jumped. It was weird in the firelight. Finally a large tray was brought in and placed before the groom. Two of his friends (recent grooms) then were deputized to henna his hands. They carefully wrapped up each hand after covering them with henna on the palms and nails only. After this ceremony we went to the bride's house where women were packed in as tight as could be. We were up front beside the bride. We played the gramophone – some dancing was done by the village girls – very pretty dips and turns and arm motions. Finally about 12 o'clock a tray was brought in and two recent brides hennaed the new bride's hands and feet. We left early as we were exhausted! The men stayed up till early morning, dancing and talking.

WEDDING DAY

The next morning all was excitement – sheep to be killed and a big feast prepared. We took a walk – visited, sang hymns – talked with some of the men – interesting and, we hope profitable discussions on religion. That afternoon the groom's friends and the gray beards of the village gathered on a rooftop for a bit of sport, and we women folk looked on from a higher roof. Presents in the form of melons, nuts, raisins, and small pieces of money were demanded from all guests, and placed before the groom – as each was brought a small boy of the giver went forward and kissed the groom three times. There was of course much banter, and talk and jesting, and dancing and gramophone music going on the whole time. Presents for the groom from the bride were carried in on a tray – new clothes which he donned for the final ceremony. At the end the fruit was passed around to all the guests. After a bit of rest the real excitement came. We walked down out the farther end of the village to the bride's uncle's house where all were gathered, men and women. There we saw another performance few, if any, have seen. In a crowded room, we sitting right up under the bride's feet, the groom was brought in and stood beside her. Her father was there – he put her hand in grooms, kissed them both – they each ate a raisin or sweet – then the groom picked up a mirror and they uncovered her face enough to let him look at her in the mirror, and then he rushed out of the room. All threw sweets at them. Then we filed out – a large and noisy procession formed, the drum and pipes playing, and we women in the rear with the bride. Several stops were made for the friends to dance a bit – prayers to be made – incense was carried thru the crowed on the heads of women relations. It was thrilling to be part of it – we wound up the hill – caught glimpses of the valley below, the distant mountains and the glories of the sunset. Before we reached the groom's house the bride's dowry, carried by several men, joined the procession. At the groom's house, his father did the same thing of joining their hands as her father had done. That night there were more parties, feasts, and dancing until late. We had another religious discussion group, and a big crowed for hymn singing! I went to bed early. The talk and requests for hymns always came from them. We did not force it on them but they wanted as much as we had strength to give.

LEAVING FOR HOME

The next day by noon the guests began to leave, but we stayed as they wouldn't let us go – just refused to give us donkeys! It really was great fun, and they couldn't have been more thoughtful or careful of our comfort to the extent of their abilities. Wednesday we had breakfast and lunch, both at another recent groom's house (the week before) interspersed with music, a walk in the fresh air, good conversation, and reading of their holy book by one of the young men. That afternoon we called on the bride in her new house (same room as Ma and Pa and daughter) more dancing, and talk, and music. In the evening, our last there, the bride was invited to her father's house – to which she cannot return until asked – for a big feast. Many of the big men of the village were asked. Men and women separate for the most part. The groom's father did the cooking, after three or four hours there the whole crowd repaired to the school and meeting house – for a final hymn singing, and how we sang. I was so hoarse and Elizabeth gave out latterly as she was getting a cold. The bride and groom escorted us home along with a few others, and it was 11:30 by then. In the morning we packed up, and I had a big clinic – writing many prescriptions and giving advice. A huge crowd came to say goodbye – bringing presents and were so kind to us. We mounted donkeys, and waved to the women – still gay in their holiday scarves of red, and the men in best store clothes, and rode down to the plains. Three accompanied us, and have insisted on staying until we find a car.

Time to stop and take a walk. No car yet, and I'm beginning to get restless. Hope you can read this. There is much more I could write.

Dec. 9, 1939

Home again – finally got a car – a truck and sat up with the chauffeur, our stuff and Gholam in back. Was it cold! Breakfast with coffee and toast and sitting on chairs was so good. Now I must pack and do final things. Also an extra special bath and hair wash. No chance for bathing or any privacy much on such a trip. I hope to leave day after tomorrow for Teheran and Resht.

It was a great trip to that village – they are really superior folk there. Ismaili's or the assassins in history – read up about them.

Much, much love
Adelaide

EXTRACTS FROM TWO RECENT LETTERS OF DOCTOR ADELAIDE KIBBE, RECOUNTING A SHORT VACATION TO PERSEPOLIS

Resht, March 4, 1940

Mails are finally coming through, and I am hearing accounts of Thanksgiving and November birthdays, and Christmas preparations and end of January doings all in the same mail.

No more news to report to you of the educational institutions. As you know, the government is taking over the schools – nothing is settled yet. The mission is going to have a difficult time placing missionaries out of a job, and reassigning appropriations, and so on – so much to be readjusted. Dr. Dodds, of New York, and Dr. Hutchins, President of Washington and Jefferson in Pennsylvania, are still in Teheran conferring.

The country is having a census taken, beginning in Teheran, the capital. Everyone had to stay in his *own home* for a day or two, and city traffic was tied up – nothing entering or leaving the city, so we heard. Our town will have its turn soon I suppose.

I have been reading up on Persian art and history and archaeology in preparation for my trip. I want to be more intelligent about Persepolis and Ispahan this time. I want to read another article or two on just Persepolis, and also shall read again 'Esther'. We hope to leave in two weeks' time.

Today is 'pay clinic' day, and this afternoon come operations. Difficult baby cases continue to come in at unusual hours – I spent Sunday afternoon on one such, and also yesterday afternoon – glad they weren't middle of the night hours, anyhow.

Ispahan, March 22, 1940

We have a few minutes to spare here, so all are letter writing. We are waiting for Dr. Shafter to come take us to the Masjid-i-Juma'h – a wonderful old mosque from the time of the Seljukes in 1000-1100 A.D., or even earlier – said to be one of the most interesting examples of early Mohammedan architecture. Yesterday he took us to see the Masjid-i-shah, and the Masjid-i-Sheikh Lutjullah, with the wonderful blue dome. The tiling on these later mosques (Shah Abba's time – 1600) is beautiful reminding one of the Grand Canyon. Dr. Pope speaks of that little gem, the Blue dome, as a 'symphony' as wonderful as any in music or poetry. In the afternoon three of us went shopping. Though it was *No Ruz* Day (New Year), we found quite a few antique shops and brass and silver shops open. When I am let loose in an antique shop it is rather hard on the purse! I do love these old Persian, and some of the new, things that are to be found.

I have begun this letter backwards for I believe I didn't tell of my going to Teheran, leaving Resht Saturday evening the 16th, I think it was. As we rode through the jungle that evening at sunset, the banks along the road were covered with blue violets and yellow primroses and the sweet fragrance of the blossoms of wild plum trees came into the car.

Teheran, March 29, 1940

To continue the story – we got to Teheran so early in the morning that we didn't want to wake up our hostesses, 4:30 a.m. – so we went out to the hospital and sat in Dr. McDowell's office, and washed, rested, ate and waited until a more reasonable hour. After three days in Teheran – for shopping and visiting and just enjoying some of things we don't have in the smaller cities, we started for the south. There were two cars of us, Ellen and Janet Frame and I from Resht, Margaret Cowden and Sylvia Sherk – a short-term teacher in Sage College – in one car with a Persian driver and a crowd of missionary kids and nurse and teacher in the other. It is about an eight to ten hour ride to Ispahan across dry, alkaline, desert country most of the way – passed a large salt lake, thru the city of Gom, sacred as the burial place of Fatimen Ma'asumeh, sister of the Imam Reza, buried in Meshed. We saw an interesting museum there – small but containing a few nice bits. We reached Ispahan that evening and found that our three Reshtis were staying with the sisters (nurses) at the English hospital – comfortable though rather chilly quarters. It is almost still winter though by rights it should be warmer.

A day and a half in Ispahan, my carload pushed on to Persepolis. We left after lunch, and rode about four hours across more desert, passed rocky mountains, and great vistas of which one sees so many in Iran. That night we lodged in a 'hotel' in a small town, which was not too bad – though some of the sheets had been slept in! We left early the next morning for Persepolis and Shiraz. We crossed a mountain range – climbing gradually and then descended to the plain where old Persepolis is found. About sixty miles this side of Persepolis, we turned off the road and were stopped by a good-sized stream of water, which the car couldn't cross. Our aim was to see Cyrus' tomb – earlier date than Darius (about 500 B.C.) located out there in that barren, isolated desert – a huge stone pile of really beautiful proportions – a few pillars surround it – rather portions of pillars and gateways, and a cemetery that is still in use by the villagers near. We walked over plowed land about a quarter of a mile or so from there, to where his palaces stood – Pasargodar, and where one sees only a few old columns and stone pavement. One column has an interesting carved human figure with wings.

After this jaunt of about four or five miles, we rode on to Persepolis. First you come to the gateway to the left of the road – massive stone blocks – later you pass a well-worn groove in the rocks that was a portion of the water system. Then a few more stone blocks that was the altar of the Fire Worshippers – another gateway that led to the bath and then, as you round a curve in the road, to the left bursts upon you the full majestic beauty of the massive stone entrance staircases and columns of Persepolis.

Since I was here in 1931, much work has been done by Dr. Herzfeld, Dr. Schmidt, and now an Iranian. Our driver had been Dr. Herzfeld's driver there at Persepolis for five and a half years, and knew a lot about the excavations in his day. He could tell us details and called our attention to interesting carvings, and so on. Look up in the *National Geographic* for 1933 on Persepolis, and perhaps other pictures of these beautiful staircases and figures thereon. We went into the museum on the place and saw bits of pottery from the Stone Age Village (7000 B.C.) near Persepolis. After spending several hours wandering around – marveling at the beauty of those mighty columns against the blue sky, the intricacy of some of the carvings, looking down the great cistern, over 140 feet, that gave water to Persepolis, seeing the drains underground, tombs on the hills back of it, and so on, we left it and went on for an hour or so to Shiraz. There we stayed at the new Saddi Hotel for Saturday and Sunday evening and left early Monday morning, back in one day to Ispahan, and after another day there and one returning to Teheran and two days here, we are off for Resht.

LIFE AS A DOCTOR

Personal Report
1939-1940

As I look back over this last year of work three words stand out, 'mothers and babies'.

Comparatively speaking perhaps we have not had so many, but there have been far more obstetrical cases this

year than for any previous annual record of either hospital
I have been in. While much is being done to make things
easier for the mother, no one does anything about babies
coming at night, which is not so easy from the doctor's
point of view! One becomes adept at answering the
telephone with only the organs of speech awake, and
dressing rapidly while still half asleep. The normal, or
nearly so, clean case is not the trouble, rather the tragic,
neglected and maltreated mothers brought in from the
villages are the true nightmares. They will continue to be
so until better midwifery training and control of midwives
is possible, and until more bed space is made available
for the unfortunate village mother. The bright spot that
lightens this midnight work is that these village women
do have remarkable powers of recovery. There have been
some real miracles performed by nature, the results of
which have been able to walk out on their own two feet.
Again one strikes a snag when they return the next year
in the same condition. I have seen three or four such
recently, and we have tried again to impress upon them
the importance of prevention rather than last minute
cure. A big field of endeavor lies there.

Strange to say my tasks are not only with the 'women
and babies' by any means, or the women's clinic, or even
the women surgical and medical inpatients. At times
throughout the year I must treat the men who come,
especially emergency cases, an operation for strangulated
hernia, or mastoiditis, or an intestinal obstruction may be
necessary perhaps even at night. Not long ago we women
of the hospital managed to a successful conclusion one of
the late night emergency cases, a tall brawny fisherman
from a town on the edge of the Caspian.

Other than hospital work I have had the pleasure of playing the hymns for the church services throughout the year. Also I have made some calls on church members.

Recently I have been taking Persian lessons again and am more impressed than ever with the fact that I have barely scratched the surface of a most interesting language study.

Ten years of life and work in Iran end this fall. I wish that I might report more accomplished in a tangible form. I try to follow where the spirit leads, and I am more sure than ever that I would rather be here and do this work than anything else, while I can.

Adelaide Kibbe.

Resht Hospital Report 1939-1940

A lad of thirteen, with a broken arm, said to me the evening I first saw him and asked how it had happened, "I was playing out in the fields and fell. It was God's will that I broke my arm …"

As I set his broken bones, I told him why I thought otherwise, that we could really not hold God to account for this accident. He did not want us to break our bones and suffer. The events of the past year in the hospital at Resht, some of which at the time may have seemed catastrophic, perhaps resulted partly from the frailties of human nature, or maybe they were evidence of God's will for us. Who can say?

PERSONNEL

Dr. Frame was at work continuously from July to April, nine months, when he left for a short furlough in America. Dr. Kibbe relieved in Meshed Hospital for the months from July to December 1939, then returned to Resht at Christmas time. So the hospital had two doctors for only three months of the year. Miss Nicholson returned from furlough the last of September 1939, and immediately took over her duties on the nursing side, which Miss Benz, during her absence, had so faithfully carried on, as well as her own work as matron. Since her death in September (1939), Mrs. Frame's place in the Baby Clinic was filled, after a two month interval, by Mrs. Browning, who has given generously of her time, despite her busy schedule...

NURSING

The Nursing Department has attracted more attention than usual this year. Early in the fall, public graduation was held in the auditorium of our Girl's School. Seven of our nurses received Government diplomas from the city Superintendent of Schools, these being among the first awarded in five schools of nursing throughout Iran.

A new Class of four started in October. These too were exceptional because for the first time, through the interest and efforts of Miss Benz, our hospital evangelist and matron, blue dresses and white aprons were made possible as uniforms for the students. To American hospitals, such a distinction is an accepted fact, but until now, for one reason or another, we have never been able to have a separate and distinct wearing apparel for our student nurses.

Our nurses are all Resht girls, going and coming each day to the hospital as we have no nurses' home. For the day sleeping of night nurses, we do have a separate room and this is appreciated because the homes of most of these girls would not permit sleeping during the day.

MISCELLANEOUS

The national personnel has remained about the same. Our druggist, Baron Tzolog dar Hagopian, had the opportunity to purchase a pharmacy and so set up in business for himself. He has, however, continued to cooperate with the hospital in a most friendly and helpful way. Since we have no registered pharmacist, we are forced to send our clinic patients outside for drugs and he is willing to dispense for us a number of our more special medicines, and to also prepare medicines for the hospital inpatients.

The X-ray, the only machine in Gilan Province, was greatly in demand this last year until spring, when trouble developed and it refused to work, much to our dismay. Fortunately, after a number of days of careful work and experimentation, Dr. Frame was able to find the cause and to remedy it, and it is again in good order. Thursday afternoons we have a regular clinic for fluoroscopy and pneumothorax for a few tuberculosis patients, for whom we feel we are accomplishing a bit in the way of arresting the disease...

In April an unfortunate death on the operating table was the cause of a lawsuit brought against Dr. Kibbe, which caused considerable excitement within and without the hospital. Up to the present, while the trouble has quieted down and every indication is that nothing more will be heard from it, it is still not entirely settled and off the books after these months. A lawyer of good repute has the case in his hands...

Respectfully submitted,
Adelaide Kibbe, M.D.

Photo 5.3 Dr. Frame in back row, Gertrude Benz, Dr. Kibbe, and Ellen Nicholson in front row

The story of the tragic event that follows is best told in the letter from Gertrude Benz, a missionary nurse, who wrote to my grandmother about what happened.

A TRAGIC DEATH

It is with Adelaide's permission I am writing you. So much has happened in this past few weeks in which Adelaide has been involved that I felt if it were me, I should appreciate someone here also writing my people. Several weeks ago, word suddenly came from the authorities here that Adelaide's registration as a doctor did not include the privilege of doing surgery. It was a slip up at the time the licenses for all doctors were issued. We learned since that her license included all so she went right on working as before, soon there was a demand of a bribe from some of the office force to which we did not agree, but referred it to Teheran where it was cleared up. All of this necessitated many trips to city officials. March 31, Adelaide returned from her trip south, a day or two later she was notified to again appear before the officials, they having heard she referred this matter to Teheran, which exposed their demands. Needless to say they were not pleased.

On April 5, while Adelaide was operating on a woman for hemorrhoids, the patient died on the table. The family and relatives who were at the hospital went wild with excitement, declaring the doctor was responsible for the patient's death. One of the sons went at once to the police and made a charge to that effect and refused burial until there was a meeting of doctors.

All the doctors met and thoroughly went over the case and exonerated her from all blame. The case could not be withdrawn because of its nature. It was then referred to the Department of Justice. We employed a lawyer but it had to go thru too many courses which meant many interviews, examinations, trips to the different offices, and so on.

All of this was of course a great strain on Adelaide, the saddest part of it all was we could help so little. My heart never before ached for anyone as it did for her those days. Yet she was brave and uncomplaining as you can well imagine. I might say here that I am expressing the opinion of all the local doctors, mission doctors and community when I say that as a doctor and surgeon Adelaide is considered one of the best in the country. Her thoroughness and conscientiousness is outstanding. This was just one of those unfortunate affairs that cannot be helped. The sympathy of the community is with Adelaide and though the case is not absolutely finished we have every assurance of the people in authority that it will be.

This of course is an unhappy episode yet it perhaps precipitated what would have doubtless eventually happened. Dr. (John) Frame did his utmost to help in every way he could, thus showing what some of us here already knew, his fondness or rather love for Adelaide. She has written you that she and he have become engaged to be married. We are glad because both seem to be very happy. I know he will love Adelaide and be kind to her and make her happy. She deserves only the best. She is a dear precious girl and worthy of all the happiness that can come to her. Dr. Frame, as you know, has been here a good many years and highly respected, a man of good principals and deep religious convictions. Adelaide was at first a bit sensitive about it happening so soon after his wife's death, yet it all seemed to happen in the past few weeks.

Who looks at Beauty

Who looks at beauty with glad eyes
And finds in it surcease from care,
Who marks each small and lovely thing,
Is praising God all unaware.

Whose heart lifts up in gratitude
For cloud and leaf and budding stem,
Is sharing the delight He knew the morning
He created them.

Whose ears are keen to catch the first
Faint bird note in the darkened trees,
Can hear the music of the spheres,
The ageless heavenly symphonies.

Who holds his breath at the far scent
Of some wild blossom on the air
Is giving thanks unknowingly
Is voicing an unspoken prayer.

Grace Nell Crowell
(John sent this to Adelaide after their engagement)

There were no letters from Adelaide to her family about her engagement in the collection of papers, so Gertrude Benz's letter to Adelaide's parents is the first reference we have about her engagement to John Frame. As they had been working together in the hospital for many years, they were already well acquainted. John had three children – John, Jr. who was just finishing medical school in Chicago, Charles, a newly appointed home missionary in Wisconsin, and Jennette (also called Janet) in high school in Teheran. The trip described in a previous letter was partially intended for Jennette to get better acquainted with Adelaide Kibbe. Jennette told me that at the time she couldn't understand why she was riding in the car with Adelaide instead of with the other kids on the trip. It wasn't until later, on the trip back to the United States, that her father told her that he was going to marry Adelaide. As her mother had died only the previous September he was concerned about her feelings towards his remarrying.

In the summer of 1940 John Frame took a short furlough to the United States to settle his daughter Jennette in high school, visit with his sons Charles and John, and talk to supporting churches of the work in Resht. Leaving Wheaton, Illinois, he traveled to California and then on to Iran via the Pacific. Extracts from his letter to his sister Margaret, a missionary in Shanghai, tells of a short visit with future in-laws in Berkeley, California. The letter also notes the difficulties of traveling across the Pacific because of rising tensions with Japan and Russia.

Dear Margaret,

...We had expected the President Taft to sail Oct. 15th and I had arranged to spend two days with Dr. Kibbe's family in Berkeley. The boat did not sail until Oct. 19th thus giving me a longer visit with them. I think we all thoroughly enjoyed the visit, Adelaide's mother was the daughter of Ira M. Condit and born in China...

The boat was delayed by local strikes. Just the time it should have sailed came the edict from Washington against women and children staying in the Orient. The official prevented two of our party, wives, from sailing with the boat because it touches at Japan but have promised to permit them to sail on the President Adams which goes direct to Manila...

It does seem too bad to get so near and not see you. But it also seems too bad to have to go all the way around via India when the route across Russia would have been so much nearer and much quicker.

With love,

John

Photo 5.4 Leaving for Iran after visiting Adelaide's family in Berkeley

When the camels have all lain down on the job

And the mules have a sit-down strike,

When the post horse no longer runs his course,

And there's not even a motor bike,

When the chauffers refuse to step on the gas,

And the trains are stuck on the track,

When the STEAMBOATS never, never sail,

And you're left along with your pack,

Remember then you can go by AIR

By air to the fairest maid,

Step into your plane, soar into the main'

And fly to your Adelaide.

Christmas greetings to the belated bridegroom
(Author unknown)

CHAPTER 6

Joys and Sorrows 1941—1944

The following letter was written by Ellen Nicholson, head nurse, to Adelaide's mother describing Adelaide and John's wedding.

A WEDDING

Resht, Iran
Jan 22, 1941

Dear Mrs. Kibbe,

Knowing that Gertrude Benz wrote to you last spring, and also that you would and did become acquainted with Dr. Frame, I have not before written. But now as one of few Resht members, you may be interested in my version of the events of the past months and particularly those of the last few weeks.

Working with Adelaide these two or three years in Meshed and Resht, meeting her several times in different capacities throughout the Mission, and travelling with her to Persepolis and back last Spring, both as a worker, as a friend and as Mission member. Since having this new joy come into her life, and being thrown on her own in the hospital, I have again seen sidelights of her character, ability and capacity to love and understand, which might never had been my privilege or taken years and years to ferret out, for Adelaide really is quite a reticent person.

As for John Frame, I can say no more than that I have been his hospital nurse for years, have seen him under all sorts of stress and strain and always with the greatest of admiration. One should know him in action as a doctor, as one who understands well the psychology of Iranians, as an executive both in hospital and as a mission member, to weigh his full worth. Personally, I was very glad to have him again establish a home and rejoice that Adelaide is the one whom he loves and who loves him with equal intensity. I am sure you understand that on the mission field, especially such a small one as Iran and Resht, we who are here get far more insight into the hearts and minds of such folks than would ever happen at home. With the mails so very irregular all the months of John's absence, Adelaide was left very much to herself. Gertrude and I helped when and where we could, but at best were but substitutes.

John probably wrote back to you along the travel route, but we at this end were always uncertain until within a week or so, just when he would reach Iran. Debating asking another Mission doctor to relieve in hospital while Adelaide was away, his arriving date was an important item. We could not have the relieving man too early; if John's arrival date was to be Christmas time, the snows of Kermanshah-Hamadan pass would block his coming and returning, in all probability. Finally we decided that I would carry on with as few patients, in hospital as possible and have an Armenian M.D. on call. How grand it was for Adelaide to receive a wire on January 7th that John was actually in Iran, even if far down on the Gulf. A couple of days brought wire from railhead, then some words from Mr. Payne assuring Adelaide that he would speed John's departure from Teheran.

All this, of course, after Adelaide decided on having the wedding in Resht. The Hoffmans especially as friends of Adelaide's and the Paynes as particular friends of John, would have so like to have had it there. Needless to say, we Reshtees, and especially I, are glad she decided on Resht. Between the arrival time element and the possible snow on roads, it would have been difficult after January 1st to have gone to Teheran.

Stopping but two hours in Teheran where he breakfasted (a record time I assure for it always is twenty-four or forty-eight hours to get necessary permissions) he wired his expected arrival at a small village deep in the gorge of the large White River (*Safid Rud*) a place famous for its olive groves. Lynn Browning (fellow missionary in Resht) rented an auto, brought it out on the boulevard (going to the garage or in front of hospital would have attracted too large a crowd) where Adelaide arrived in a carriage and she was off for about a two-hour ride. They made excellent connections, she arriving a little ahead of him. The day was warm and sunny for January 11th, no snow. The baggage came on to my gate in John's car – they tarried an hour or so. You see if they were to marry quietly and get away for a while, it needed to be done without the general population knowing about the matter. There naturally was general interest about town in the arrival of the long-looked for and famous Dr. Frame and also his marriage to Dr. Kibbe. We did not even tell our servants that *this* was to be the day. If the wedding was not strictly private, a great crowd of church, hospital people and friends of long standing would feel terribly slighted otherwise.

After Adelaide got away to Rudbar, Gertrude and I looked over my potted plants and those of the Frames for potential decorations. My smallish living room was to be fixed up for the occasion. Adelaide all along had thought it would well adapt itself and I believe that it did.

The station library and my own books line most of two walls; the three doors and two wide windows (it is a native build house) are covered with long, reddish-blue *galamcars*, (material with block printing), soft tones, made years ago. The best touch is the fireplace, wide and low, the nicest in Resht, I believe. Closing off one of the doors, we stood two tall plant stands on either side. On these we placed heavy pots of large, wiry, droopy, ferns. To one side was a double-deck *tachcheh*, (built in niches). These two spaces were filled with greenish plants, there being two tall pink geraniums among the lot. The other side of this corner was the fireplace. In the deep center of the large window at the other end of room, framed by *galamcars*, was a large basket of ferns with a few red roses and narcissus scattered through. This was given by our local flower grower, whose daughter manages our surgery. Above the fireplace were two heavy red candles and a vase containing two lovely full-bloom roses, the last from a special bush in my yard. The fireplace was lighted early to permit burning well down to glowing coals. This and the light from one large floor lamp was sufficient. From the same gardener we were able to get the last of the December violets, a creditable sized bouquet which we tied with silver ribbon and Adelaide wore on the lovely pink dress.

Adelaide has probably told you they arrived about 6 p.m., opened up the suitcase at my place, tried on the dress, the slip, shoes, and so on. The slip needed shortening; then she went over, had tea with John and back to bathe and dress at my place, leaving John in full possession of the servant and facilities over there. Were we all excited! Gertrude sewing and pressing all necessary things, even John's suit was sent over, not having been well packed. I watched the fireplace and various stoves in as many rooms, kept an ear open for knocks at the door, ran over to hospital to see that all was quiet as we did not want the staff to know it was taking place just at that hour. Adelaide brought the wedding ceremony used by Dr. Hunter, which you all signed. Lynn Browning was looking this over carefully, deciding whether the light would be sufficient for him over in the corner. The Scotch bank people, Millars, were due any time and I kept the one man near that door. John came over with odd bits he had brought for the Brownings; as all was not ready he went back for more, calendars, and so on. Adelaide got ready and still no Millars. What could be keeping them? Finally we telephoned from hospital and received no answer. After waiting five minutes more to give them time to arrive if they had just left, we went on with the ceremony without them. So you see there were but Mrs. Browning, Miss Wilder (a new person in our midst), Miss Benz and me. Next day we found that the Millars had misunderstood the last note, had been sitting all hatted at home awaiting *another* final word. Their phone as often happens, had not rung at all.

Adelaide was truly a beautiful bride. Her short hair was in a nice wave, excitement adequately supplied color. During her responses there was a tremor in her voice, but this added to the solemnity and made our hearts go out to her. Lynn Browning is at his best in these formal occasions. Adelaide had requested that he not use the printed prayers, but his own thoughts and they were fittingly beautiful this night. After John had emphatically kissed the bride, we all had an opportunity and we then sat a few minutes while I passed around the American chocolates brought over by John, a gift from Adelaide's sister. Soon the couple went back to their house across the wall, we carried over a supper tray to the front hall, together with the suitcases and all the bride's leftover clothes. By 9:30 Sunday morning an auto came for them at my door and they were off for a well-earned time together.

Returning the 20th, Gertrude and I supervised a general reception for them in their own house on Tuesday. The graduate nurses, with Gertrude's help, made the cakes and served the tea to the guests. Needless to say the nurses were very pleased to be permitted this honor. Although we had but a day to send around verbal notices, we had all we could handle between four and seven p.m. from church people in all walks of life, to all the hospital fold, all the city's doctors and some of their wives, representatives of the police and detective departments and some of their many friends – serving tea and cake to more than this hundred, keeping the crowd moving to make room for others, estimating whether sweets would be sufficient, and so on, were the responsibilities of the rest of us. Adelaide and John must have been thoroughly tired after greeting and talking to so many, but they carried it all through in an adequate way.

Now they are both back in the hospital, ostensibly as usual, but with a fine new comradeship, as colleagues, yes, but what is bigger and closer, man and wife. Personally, I hope A. does not try to carry on the same full hospital lead for long. She owes it to herself, to John and to the home they have established, to spend some quiet hours therein, simply planning the living. I too will be sorry to have her drop much hospital work, especially the surgery in which she has always been efficient and in these latter times quite fearless and *very* successful. She has a large clientele right here in Resht where she is new. And the nurses simply adore her, will do anything, anytime, if I only assign them tasks working along with 'Dr. Kibbe' as she will be yet for a long while.

Through the years these two in their spheres have been a force for Jesus Christ in this land. Now with their added interest, their new consecration, their devotion to one another and to the Cause, I know they will go onward and forward to greater things in the years just ahead. Such is my prayer for them.

I trust you received the cable promptly. The telegraph office here were difficult to convince that San Francisco was a city, declared California sufficient as an address. It seems San Francisco is not printed in their guide.

May this letter find you, your husband and rather large American family in the best of health. I would like to take this opportunity to extend my hearty and sincere good wishes to you both on the fiftieth anniversary of *your* marriage which I understand comes during April. May the Lord continue to bless you and your house.

Sincerely,
Ellen D. Nicholson

THE YEAR IN RETROSPECT

Mission Report
1941

On some one of the various documents recently necessary, my occupation was put down as physician, surgeon, and housewife. These three words quite adequately describe my work during the past year. Let us read between the lines, and enlarge briefly upon the three words.

For the first six months of the year I was physician surgeon only as I have been for nearly twelve years here in Iran, endeavoring to give my first thoughts to the needs there. As I was the only doctor in the station during those months I carried on as best I could under the circumstances. The law case of the previous April was still hanging fire, and continued to cause me not a little inward perturbation. Finally in October it was successfully settled and I was again a free woman. I accepted mostly women and children as patients, though some men continued to come to me for treatment (such) as hernias, abscesses, and so on. There were always a few men inpatients on hand, too. Despite the lawsuit over my head, and being alone for both diagnosis and the actual technical aspects of the operation, I felt it necessary to do as much surgery as I possibly could, for surgeons in Resht are scarce.

In January, after much delay and uncertainty, Dr. Frame finally arrived in Resht, and then I added housewife to my previous occupation of physician and surgeon. After a short holiday in the middle of January we started again in the hospital on a two doctor basis. Thus far I have put practically full time in the hospital so that the three words correctly represent my tasks for the second half of the year.

In retrospect it has not been an easy year, full responsibility toward the hospital even though more than ably upheld by Miss Nicholson and Miss Benz, decisions to make alone and uncertainties for the future marked the first six months. With Dr. Frame's return, work in the hospital began to flow more smoothly and naturally for me as physician and surgeon. And also with his return my joys and trials as housewife are just beginning.

Respectfully submitted,
Adelaide Kibbe Frame

Photo 6.1
Dr. John Davidson Frame, 1941

Photo 6.2
Adelaide playing the organ – Resht 1941

Personal Report
J.D. Frame
June 30, 1941

The beginning of the (report) year found me at home visiting the children and friends, making arrangements for Jennette's school life. The furlough though short was a satisfactory one. The chief anxiety became, toward the end, when and how to return to Iran. The only route available was via the Pacific and in order to get a suitable sailing I cut short my intended furlough by two weeks.

The journey itself consumed just three months. The boats were slow; there were delays for connections in Manila and Bombay; delays for loading freight in Hong Kong, Singapore and Penang; brief stops in Hawaii, Japan and Columbo. Christmas day in Bombay was spent with a house party, which included some old Wooster friends.

After a tedious delay in Bombay we finally started up the Persian Gulf. Landing in Khorremshahr we made the trip to Teheran by the new and very fine railroad, a truly scenic route.

Ordinarily the traveler is delayed in Teheran 24 hrs., or more, for passes. Here, however was the one place on the trip where we made better time than expected. Mr. Payne had arranged with an old friend of mine in the police department to expedite matters so that a pass was issued immediately after my arrival and I was on the way out of Teheran within three hours. Dr. Kibbe met me forty miles out, we returned to Resht together and were married that evening, Jan. 11. We spent eight days in Ramasar and then took up medical work once more.

Having been absent less than nine months and that within the fiscal year, Dr. Kibbe, now Mrs. Frame, and I soon found ourselves back in the old familiar routine in the hospital. The hospital had been running almost as usual during the whole time of my absence, the chief difference being in reduced numbers of men in the wards and in dispensary. The flouroscopic and pneumothorax service had definitely increased. As a matter of fact, even now I have not caught up with Mrs. Frame in the numbers of outpatients seen, nor the inpatients requiring serious surgery.

If the hospital work slipped smoothly back into routine, life outside the hospital was something new and different! The joy of establishing a home, however important and absorbing as it is to the individual, is scarcely the expected theme of such a report as this.

Respectfully submitted,
J. Davidson Frame

LETTER TO MARGARET FRAME, JOHN'S SISTER, LIVING IN CHINA

Resht, August 3, 1941

Margaret A. Frame
American Presbyterian Mission, Shanghai, China

Dear Margaret,
    Adelaide and I have just returned from two weeks' vacation in Hamadan and Mission meeting in Tabriz

... Adelaide not being a delegate did not attend all the sessions, especially after she was appointed to write the mission narrative. I tell her that though not a delegate she is probably more conversant with the work of the mission than any of the delegates.

The two most serious problems before the mission did not require immediate answer but took considerable time and thought. One was the probable necessity of closing a hospital within a year unless there is some definite reinforcement. Dr. McDowell has resigned and one or two of us are approaching retirement age. A number of furloughs also all fall due in 1944. The Board is trying to send Dr. Newman from China to carry on here but it is still very uncertain whether he will secure the necessary visas, and so on, especially since the latest news from your part of the world.

The other problem was responsibility for deciding when evacuation might be necessary, the extent to which it should be carried out and who should remain till the last possible moment in each possible contingency. The latest news, or rather the lack of definitive news, leads us to hope that the necessity may not arise at all. But you may have some quite different news about the situations, which will affect us even before this letter reaches you.

When we returned we found quite a pile of mail here including three letters from yourself. Your letters apparently all come via the south instead of across Siberia as you hoped. I am sending this in duplicate hoping the Russian route will still be available to a properly addressed letter.

Sometimes there is a feeling that our medical working is becoming unnecessary because of the development of

local health services in some form or other, but this past
month, when we closed the hospital entirely, seems to
have demonstrated that in certain lines we still hold the
fort. Perhaps next year we will arrange for Adelaide to
spend a month or more at Pahlavi near the sea and I will
come back and forth a couple of times a week so that it
will not be necessary to close the hospital entirely. This
year however gave us an opportunity of having it painted
while we were away and gave Miss Benz a free hand
in getting the newly arrived material for linens worked
up into sheets, garments, and so on. It also allowed us
to give our somewhat depleted staff vacations all at one
time so that we will not be stumbling shorthanded when
in operation.

Although railroads are increasing in Iran, travel
is still somewhat strenuous especially over the routes
which we have had to travel. Adelaide and I decided
to take a car at our own expense rather than travel in
the autobus, which had been chartered for the party.
We drove from 6 a.m. to 9 p.m. the first day with
only a brief stop for lunch. The hotel in Kazvin is
not comfortable, not as well furnished as many now to
be found, but it did afford some slight rest. In Kazvin
one has to wait for a chance seat in a car passing from
Teheran to Resht. Such a car turned up at 2 p.m. and
we were home about 10 p.m. Baths were ready and
we turned into bed with only melon for supper. Friday
we loafed and got organized, Saturday went back to
the hospital. Mr. Browning had come on by bus
and freight train and again bus with two nights en
route and was so knocked out that I took his service
for him this morning. Adelaide and I feel somewhat
stiff even yet from the trip, but have decided that what

we need perhaps is a little walk and will say goodbye with love from us both.

John

Photo 6.3 Margaret Frame – John's sister

ADVENT OF THE X-RAY MACHINE

August 18, 1941

Dear Friends,

...For a long time we have reached the maximum of effort or expansion which our time and equipment will permit. These changes which come are now more subtle. They lie rather in the quiet demand for better service, the willingness to accept more difficult operations, the realization that in X-ray there are new means of diagnosis.

Sometimes the demands of our patients still run beyond our ability and often they expect strange things of us. For instance, only this morning I had a patient who had come over a hundred miles to see me because of consequences of chronic malaria. There was nothing startling or dramatic which I could do. He needs persistent tonic treatment. He was much disappointed that I did not use the X-ray to confirm the obvious diagnosis, or reveal something which was not obvious, and further disappointed that I did not insist he stay in the city while I gave him a long course of injections which are the great 'piece de resistance' of the ordinary doctor in Iran.

The fact that our medical work runs along more or less routinely in a somewhat set pattern does not mean that we do not have very serious problems, which take thought and time. The war has naturally cut off supplies and means of communication – note please the date you receive this letter! – and already caused a shortage of medical needs. Recognizing the dangers of the situation the Board authorized us to order two years supplies in advance. These have just recently come to hand and we are rejoicing in our full storeroom and new linens, and so on. There remains however the matter of paying for them! Exchange has risen so that it will take three or four times as much to pay for them in local currency as in previous years and all our budgets and accounts as well as regular appropriations are in local currency! The Board has recognized this problem also and made some special dollar appropriations. For ourselves therefore we are settled for a long pull.

The next question is as to whether we will be permitted to carry on for this period. There has been no indication that the Government expects to take over our hospitals as they did the schools, but I have no doubt that you have already read in the papers, or heard rumors over the radio, indicating that our privilege of staying may be cut off by forces from outside the land itself. Just when or how these may reach us is not, of course, very obvious. We carried on through the last war in spite of rumors and various invasions here and there into this land.

With all this uncertainty one sometimes wonders just what we are accomplishing. It is good these days to have an obvious and immediate task and to realize that if we do this well we are making our best contribution for the coming regeneration of this land and others which we hope and expect will follow all this turmoil. Since the schools have been closed there have been more workers free to seek opportunities with personal contacts with a wider range of individuals and to undertake some work for special under privileged or less accessible groups. In looking over the reports from our missionaries recently, I was interested to see how much was being done for social extremities. Seeking to help the poor in various ways and carrying on contacts with former students in our schools, both those still in the schools which the government has taken over and those who had graduated in former years.

Here in our hospital, Miss Gertrude Benz, who has been acting as housekeeper for us while carrying on evangelistic work for women, is developing constantly widening contacts with patients and is organizing more social service work to help the poor mothers who bring their children to the Baby Clinic. It is always a problem to utilize to the fullest the contacts which the hospital affords.

This is true of all our medical work. Some of you may recall that for many years I made efforts to develop an outstation work in Lahijan, visiting the city myself, establishing there a druggist at one time and later a medical evangelist. There has not been much to show for the work done in these past years. Today, however, there are two patients in the hospital with whose families I have had former contact in many ways over in Lahijan. One came for a rather simple condition; the other, with wide connections in the army, for a serious emergency operation. One wonders what the ultimate effect of these contacts will be upon the ideals and life of the patients and their friends.

As I indicated above, this letter will come to many of you with our Christmas greetings and too all it carries our best wishes for the New Year.

Most Sincerely,
J. Davidson Frame

A BABY ON THE WAY

September 28, 1941

Margaret A. Frame
American Presbyterian Mission,
Shanghai, China

Dear Margaret,
We have been so fortunate to receive several letters from you this last week or so – it does seem good to hear

from one's own as recently as August! We feel rather cut off and isolated as you do, too, I should judge, and we certainly feel uncertain and unsettled! I suppose you hear the radio daily and know as much as we do of our own affairs here!

But whatever happens, John has decided I really ought to go to Teheran for the event in November. So that means I must leave in about two weeks time. I have saved several things of sewing to do to keep me occupied while waiting! I shall stay with the Hoffmans, with whom I was in Meshed for eight years – glad it can be old friends. I shall go prepared to evacuate, if necessary, but still *hoping* to return here at least a week or two before Christmas! It is heart breaking to think of having to leave our home and garden and hospital – maybe! If it should be so I am going to try to wait for John in some place and not get too far ahead or separated from him. I just can't conceive of being left alone with a new baby without him – cheerful talk for a letter.

I am still working in the hospital for I want to keep busy – though I must stop in a week or so to get ready. (I often wonder if and when I will ever begin again.) It has been a happy time since our marriage – working together and sharing our problems and troubles and funny happenings of the day. But the new adventure before us promises to be equally happy and satisfying. Perhaps by spring I shall not be able to keep away from a bit of work over there.

We are always so interested in your social events, your Jewish refugees and your work. I surely hope we can be together in 1944, if not sooner! Our social events were a birthday party last Friday and the four Brownings and Grace Weller for dinner today! The 'piece de resistance' today was a fruit cup with pineapple and a maraschino cherry - thought we might as well eat them and not leave them for the soldiers!

> With much love to you,
> Adelaide

A WAITING GAME

Teheran, October 22, 1941

Margaret A. Frame,
American Presbyterian Mission, Shanghai, China

Dear Margaret,

You will see that I have changed my address and am up here in the capital city waiting (im)patiently for the little one to come. While I probably came up here a little sooner than was absolutely necessary, it may be best to have done so for roads and communications might be cut off unexpectedly. I would much preferred to have remained in Resht and find it hard to wait for the necessary three weeks, more or less, until time is up[11]. Fortunately I am feeling quite well on the whole and all seems to be normal, so there should be no cause for unusual concern. John has to be alone and care for self and house outside of working hours. He writes he has been kept quite busy, too, with extra work.

---

11   There was a slight miscalculation on the part of the doctor. Margaret didn't arrive until December.

I'm staying here with Dr. and Mrs. Hoffman – out at
the hospital. I was associated with them in Meshed for my
eight years there, so feel I am among real friends. They are
very hospitable and kind and all is most comfortable and
easy for me. But I am having difficulty keeping occupied
– as I feel rather useless and let down after years of active
work! Fortunately I have some sewing for the baby, though
I am not a natural seamstress or clever with my needle –
it is all an effort for me. I had a dressmaker make some
little slips and dresses out of some fine handkerchief linen
given me and I am trying a bit of feather stitching, lace,
and so on, for decoration. (Operating is easier than that!!)
Have also some crocheting to do around an afghan I made
with 'weave it' squares, diapers to hem. So with writing
and reading and some social life I keep busy.

Saturday we had lunch with American Minister and
his wife at the Legation – Dreyfuss[12] is their name. They
are very friendly with us missionaries, on the whole. It was
a pleasure to have such a delicious lunch and served so
beautifully, too. They have fixed up the Legation also in a
very artistic way – using *beautiful* Persian things – antique
– as well as from other countries where they have been. I
believe she has plenty of money as it would take a lot to
collect the many things of real worth which she has there.

Last eve – rather late afternoon – we went to a Sibelius
Symphony concert tea – a gramophone with radio pick

---

12   Louis G. Dreyfuss, Jr. began his career in the American Consular
         Service in 1914 in Budapest, continuing to serve in numerous countries
         as Minister and Ambassador until his retirement in 1951. His last
         posting was as Ambassador to Afghanistan from 1949 - 1951. In many
         of the countries where he served, he and his wife would be personally
         involved in supporting local charitable organizations. They gave me a
         silver baby cup which I later passed on to my grandchildren.

up arrangement, which was really quite enjoyable. One of our young missionary children recently from Robert's College in Istanbul, gave us a delightful commentary on the score and showed us, or rather picked out, the themes that made up the whole.

The political situation has quieted down here. Russian and English troops have left the city. The curfew at 10 p.m. still holds, also military law. But we all have our eyes on the conditions to the north of us – perhaps nothing to affect us until spring – if then.

John enclosed a letter from you of June 28th – but we have already had one written in August! He has been writing to me every day – or nearly so which is a great comfort – for I miss my house and husband! He is a very dear person, as you know. We certainly hope circumstances will permit us to carry on our life and work there in Resht.

With loving good wishes to you,
Adelaide

JOHN'S ILLNESS

Resht, February 25, 1942

Margaret A. Frame
American Presbyterian Mission, Shanghai, China

Dear Margaret,
Thoughts of you are much in our minds, as well as your name on our tongues, these days! Wee Margaret is lying in

the Morris chair with her bottle propped up so she can suck water while moving her hands around – at least she waves one hand and 'holds' the bottle with the other.

This letter started out to speak of you, but I got off into little Margaret, for naturally she is uppermost in my thoughts these days! You know we are very anxious to hear of your whereabouts and can only hope and pray you are in comparatively comfortable and safe quarters and well fed![13] I wonder *when* we will get news. One thinks – who will be next – where will the blow fall this time?

John has been writing you regularly – in hopes that some letters will get through to you. So you probably have heard of our winter's events – quite eventful for the Frame family. And how happy we were to get back to our own home and garden and servants, and John has been improving so steadily and rapidly here. He was a fine and faithful convalescent for a month, and what's more, people of the city did *not* bother him for medical help either. They knew how seriously ill he had been and respected his need for time to recuperate. He certainly has a place in the hearts of Resht folk. Now for a week he has been back at work in the hospital and seems to be standing the increasing demands on his strength and time very well. Of course he is thankful to have recovered as rapidly as he did and to be at work again.

(I am taking for granted you have received earlier letters – knew that he had a recurrence of his old stomach

---

13   After 8 December 1941, and the attack on Pearl Harbor, the Japanese entered and occupied the British and American controlled parts of the Shanghai International Settlement. They sent European and American citizens to be interned at the Lunghua Civilian Assembly Center, or placed under house arrest.

trouble, developed uncontrollable vomiting and was taken to Teheran the day Margaret arrived!)

My time, for the present, is given over to Margaret's care, that and trying to eat enough to feed us both! So far I have succeeded and seem to be in a fair way to continue for some time. I do want to keep her milk supply always on hand just in case something should 'break' this spring – no canned milk or prepared foods are available for sudden travel! So I am not working in the hospital but trying to adjust myself, from being a busy doctor to a mother of a tiny babe. Perhaps if all goes well I can arrange for two or three hours' work in the dispensary mornings after a month or two. I rather feel I would like to work that much in the hospital – keep my hand in and help John a bit if I can. Margaret comes first, though I don't want to lose touch and forget my medicine entirely. I must confess that though a doctor, I know very little of the practical side of caring for a baby! I am gradually learning the tricks of the new profession. John is a great help.

Tonight John and I have asked Ellen N. to come in to stay with Margaret. First we are going to an evangelistic meeting at the church. I am playing the hymns for the six meetings. Then, we are going to call on the head of the Department of Justice and his wife – a patient of mine, and later John did a cesarean on her. So we shall dress up in our best and not feel we are over dressing as we would in the more modest homes. I have worn the clothes John brought out last year so very little! Now I suppose they are outmoded, though I guess new styles aren't so important these days as some other things. My cute little blue hat with a veil which sits on one side of my head seems silly to me, maybe I'll get enough courage to wear it. I have a nicely cut blue dress with blue bolero trimmed in braid, too. A brown jersey is too small for me this year much to my sorrow! I'm afraid my pretty rose wedding dress is too, though I never have a chance to wear that.

The radio is going now and Margaret has decided her bottle isn't interesting anymore. So I shall say goodbye to you after this family chat.

With love from us all and a sweet little kiss from Margaret and I think she would give you a smile, too. She did for me as I looked at her now.

Adelaide

Photo 6.4 Family at home in Resht, 1942

LETTER TO IN-LAWS

Resht,
March 8, 1942

Dear Father and Mother (Kibbe),

A long time ago I received a letter from Mother addressed just to myself but have never answered it. I thought I would do so last autumn while Adelaide was in Teheran. When she first left there was an unusual amount of medical work, which fell to my lot and later as she has doubtless reported I myself was taken ill. During my convalescence I did not seem to have either the pep or the ideas to form a letter. I neglected even the children for some weeks.

I think the slow, irregular mails also sort of take away the zest of the occasional correspondence as it does of regular letter writing. When one realizes that a letter will not only take a long time en route, being delayed here and there and then perhaps turn up with several others, there is the inclination to cease writing regularly. In recent years it has generally been possible to get letters home most quickly through my sister via the Russian route. Since the war has started we have, of course, heard nothing from her, but as Russia and Japan are not at war yet we hope the mail route is still open and that perhaps if we write to her she will receive the letters wherever she may be, we presume interned somewhere. It is casting bread upon the waters with a vengeance as it may be years before we even know whether or not she has received the letters.

I suppose the only piece of information I have to give that Adelaide will not give is to try to express how very well satisfied I am with your daughter as a wife! We have had a very full and delightful time together getting on to 14 months now. I am hoping that it will have been some satisfaction to you in these times of uncertainty to know that she is not quite alone. Naturally her own thoughts are very much with little Margaret though she has not neglected me in any way. (We certainly hope the telegram of Margaret's birth reached you though it will be some time yet before we can hear your reaction.) For the present Adelaide is not attempting any medical work but has it in mind to go back to the hospital for a few hours a day as soon as the weather warms up and we get the maid trained to look out for Margaret. More especially when we get her trained to let Margaret alone even if she does cry a little.

To go back to the excitement of last autumn we are sorry that our Mission Secretary felt that he must send a cable to the Board before he could hear from Resht. We do hope that you did not worry a great deal. We must realize that more may happen before long again. We are hoping of course that the much talked of spring drive will not reach us, but are prepared to move on if there is danger of its doing so. It seems difficult to realize that after living here in Resht over 36 years through local revolutions, the world war, various Russian occupations, and so on, I may have to move on at last. This house has been my home for longer than any other houses in my life and Adelaide seems to have come, even in this short time, to consider it is her permanent home as well. We go ahead planning the garden and the house furnishings as though we were to be permanent. (In the early years when we were living in rented quarters and must change frequently, I learned that the only way to have a home is to accept each location as though it were to be permanent and make the best of it). In the hospital we are fortunate in having a good stock of supplies and therefore can carry on there almost normally for a long time. In the meantime we hear that the American Red Cross is sending supplies this way and therefore we may be able to carry on indefinitely – unless interrupted by unfavorable events from the north.

Of course with war drawing closer around us various difficulty regarding supplies of daily living may arise, but I doubt whether we will ever get as hard pressed as we were in the last war. The government here is better organized and I think our neighbors are more interested in keeping up the morale of the people in opposition to other propaganda so that we ought not to suffer greatly. Another item is that more things are manufactured in the country now than before – sugar, cotton goods, some woolen goods and we have more and more up to date flour mills. There has been a shortage of sugar and of wheat during the past few months but even these items are coming in better now. Sugar and piece goods are rationed.

It is hard also to believe that you folks are also living in a potential war zone. We hope that it will never become an actual zone of combat.

With love to you both,
John

EXCERPTS OF LETTERS TO FAMILY IN CHINA AND CALIFORNIA

Resht
March 8, 1942

Miss Margaret A. Frame
American Presbyterian Mission, Shanghai, China

Dear Margaret,

This is going to be a hasty and uncorrected note as I am writing before breakfast for a mail which is supposed to close before nine o'clock. I had fully expected to write to you yesterday afternoon, but I slept more heavily and longer after lunch than usual, was groggy when I awoke and was then called to the hospital just as I was about to start writing

Speaking of my sleeping yesterday and last night, I find the hospital work still something of a drag even though it has not been as heavy as normal (I have tried to keep it down), but I have not had very good afternoon naps and even an occasional off night so this was an accumulative make up of sleep.

I wonder whether you have any opportunity of listening to the radio and what news you can pick up. We are waiting here of course to see what the spring will bring to us. There are so few spots untouched as yet throughout the world that we have little real hope that our life here will go on entirely undisturbed, and yet we do cling to the hope that we may be left to live here indefinitely. We are going ahead with the garden and other plans on that basis at least.

I have also mentioned some of our rationing problems. This past week we got sugar rations at last. A friend in the government has also made us some presents of loaf sugar (the ration is granulated) and has promised some granulated sugar for the hospital. We operated on his wife in emergency one evening and he has proven one of the most grateful of all our patients and is in a position to show his gratitude generously.

With love from us both,
John
J. Davidson Frame

Resht
March 15, 1942

Miss Margaret Frame
American Presbyterian Mission,
Shanghai, China

Dear Margaret,

During the past week we have received quite a bit of second class mail of various sorts but only one letter from America by sea post.

Next Saturday is the Iranian New Year. Always before that time we have fewer patients in the hospital. My inpatient work therefore has been low. I am just as willing although we do need the income. I find I tire still more quickly than I should and I am a little loath to undertake any long or difficult operation – not because of physical tiring, but for fear I will also be tired mentally and not make right decisions in any difficult problem which arises.

We are going right ahead, you see, planning for a long residence here. We got so stirred up last autumn without cause that it is possible we have reacted the other way and sit too confidently at present. Time only will tell!

Little Margaret is doing well; Adelaide is well and I feel that I am gaining.

We all send love,
John
J. Davidson Frame

American Hospital

Resht
March 18, 1942

Dearest Family,

There was no letter from you, though, which I was hoping would come – long overdue, your last being Oct. 25th. I did have a letter from Margaret in Shanghai written Dec. 15th, which was reassuring as to her comfort and present condition of living – 'considerate' and 'expect adequate adjustments'; apparently in financial difficulties though, and not much work at the office job, so that she intends to take up language study. She received our telegram (cablegram) of Margaret's arrival and was so happy to hear from her family at that time, the very beginning of trouble. I am so eager to have your letter telling of the cablegram.

We get on about the same here. John is feeling quite well on the whole, though he tires easily, I think, and does not have much reserve strength over that needed for the day's activities. Just now he is busy with end-of-the-year hospital accounts – a mean job in my estimation and one I cannot help him with, except to add columns occasionally.

March 24

We were quite thrilled today to have your airmail letter of Jan. 1st come in – do try it again for it got here finally and certainly quicker than regular service. Two sentences had been deleted (cut out) by the censor. We could make out the meaning though – seemed harmless enough!

But I was terribly sorry to hear our cablegram, sent as soon after Margaret's birth as was possible (the next morning), has never arrived. What a blow and how anxious you must have been. I am all for sending another immediately, but John figured up you would just about be getting my letters written while I was still in the hospital now, and another wire might not be news after all. Too bad, indeed, it happened so.

Today is Mohammedan New Year's Day, a big and happy holiday for all. John called on the Governor this a.m. (always a routine for the first day) and we made two other calls this late morning and then had dinner at the best local hotel, as the cook is off. This afternoon I made three more calls. Tomorrow we go together and one place I shall take baby. As you may remember the New Year's holidays really drag out for 13 days. The 13th being a special day for going out of your house and into the fields and gardens for a picnic and stroll with the family, not a bad custom, if the weather is possible.

We are wishing we could do something to trace the package of baby clothes – but I suppose they are in the hands of the gods! It would be *grand* if they did get here, though we do have to pay customs.

We all send our dearest love to each one of you,
Adelaide

Resht, Iran, April 12, 1942

Miss Margaret A. Frame
American Presbyterian Mission,
Missions Bldg Shanghai

Dear Margaret,

...While one of the Persian members of the session preaches often, he never preaches on short notice. As a consequence I took the sermon although I had missed one day during the week just because I felt too tired to go to the hospital in the morning. It is very hard to know how to limit the work especially the outpatient work. No matter what number we agree on there are always urgent cases, reports on former cases and one thing and another to add up. One cannot cut the number too low or the hurt feelings from refusals will be more injury to the work perhaps than closing up altogether.

Did I tell you that the Executive Committee had decided to close Hamadan hospital unless some relief came shortly? I had feared it might be Resht. Hamadan has protested and we are making a last effort for finding the funds and a national who will take up regular work in one of the hospitals. I have been on the Medical Committee and am chairman now. It is hard to know what to offer.

I was happy to know that you were reading Dickens. I always have wished that I enjoyed him and Shakespeare more to fill in gaps when one is ill or has idle time from other reasons. Adelaide and I have been reading aloud a few books which we had read before, but most of our reading comes from the magazines which still come through, especially the *Saturday Evening Post...*

With a great deal of love from us both,
John

DEATH OF JOHN FRAME

An Appreciation of Dr. John Davidson Frame

With a feeling of great personal loss and deep sorrow, we write of the sudden death of Dr. John Davidson Frame in Resht on Jun 11th. Although he had a severe illness in December, he became better and stronger, resuming much of the hospital work, but after a two week's illness, during which time he seemed to make progress, he suddenly was taken.

Dr. Frame was born on June 26, 1880, a son of a Presbyterian minister whose three children all went to the mission field. Murray, to China where he died after a few years of service; Margaret, also to China where she is even now working in Shanghai, and John to Iran...

In 1916 he married Grace Jennette Murray, a Resht missionary. They had four children. John D. Jr., now an intern at Cook County Hospital, Chicago; Charles Ryburn, now a home missionary among the lumber men of Minnesota, and Ellen Jennette, who attends the academy in Wheaton, Illinois. Murray died at two years of age here in Resht. Mrs. Frame also died here on September 11, 1939.

In January 1941 Dr. Frame's marriage to Dr. Adelaide Kibbe, a co-worker, again gave him a home, companionship and a zestful outlook for the future. To this union was born Margaret Adelaide on December 9th.

While Dr. Frame's primary work in Iran was as a physician and surgeon, his interests were most varied and versatile. No problem or task could dismay him. Itineration made a special appeal to him and through the early and middle years he regularly visited local bazaars about Gilan, opening a drug room and dispensary in Lahijan when his visits meant an all-night or an all-day ride on horseback. Today throughout this district, his name is a password for travelling missionaries. Although by this itineration the continuity of his Resht medical work was greatly interrupted, he felt the importance of the evangelistic and outfield medical service...

But Resht itself has greatly benefitted through these thirty-seven years by the clear insight and long-range planning and executive ability of Dr. Frame. He had the faculty of discerning latent potentialities in unpromising people, to the extent that when teaching, he inspired them to become responsible and efficient workers.

Gardening was perhaps his avocation. This hospital compound and his yard were beauty spots of Resht.

He was always trying new and better varieties for the soil of Gilan about whose flora and fauna he was an authority. But his versatility extended to such things as wiring of the hospital in odd minutes when electricity first came and the budget would not permit payment for installation. The departmental phones too were his particular handiwork in odd minutes. Not even the telephone men knew how to co-ordinate the multiple wires and make them work. Who other in Resht could set up and keep in repair the X-ray machine, taking it apart coil by coil to find the fault, or direct the building of a sliding up-right-fluoroscopy screen holder?

During the other World War when there was fighting in the vicinity and British, Russian and the Jangalies were about Resht, Dr. Frame often was attending surgeon in all camps. Later when famine and refugee conditions were so bad that Near East Relief started here, he was the doctor in charge of a large, sprawling hospital and responsible for a great encampment for refugees. Russian and Armenian speaking practical nurses were the only available assistants.

We of Mission wish to assure our deepest sympathy to his wife here in Resht, to his sons, John and Charles and daughter Jennette in America, to Florence Murray of Hamadan and Charles Murray who worked so long in this land, as well as his sister Margaret Frame in far off Shanghai, and the many other relatives and the host of friends and co-workers here and in America.

Respectfully submitted,

Members of Resht Station
June 30, 1942.

When John's health deteriorated significantly at the end, Adelaide moved him to the hospital where he could have better attention and care while she carried on the hospital work. Dr. Hoffman came down from Teheran at her request when it became obvious John was dying. By the time Dr. Hoffman arrived in Resht, John had died. The official death certificate says cause of death was perforated ulcers, for which he had been previously treated. Adelaide later consulted with Dr. John Frame, Jr. and they felt that the symptoms were more likely pancreatic cancer rather than the official diagnosis on the death certificate.

August 21, 1942

Dear Adelaide,

This morning the word came through Mr. Abbott of the death of John on June 11th in Resht. I shall try several ways to get letters through to you, but at best it will be months before you hear. You will know, however, without any letter, that my heart is aching in sympathy with you and your wee daughter. I pray she may be spared to always be a comfort and a challenge and a joy to you. Your letters have been so full of joy in your home and in John with whom you made it, that I am sure even in this great sorrow you are grateful for all the richness of these two years. I hope I may all the more seem a sister as we share this great sorrow. In these last year's John has been very close to me as he has tried to share more of his thoughts with me, and then these last months when he knew I was cut off from general correspondence you and he have been so very good about writing that I have felt very close to your little family and the letters have meant more than in ordinary times. It will be sometime before I can hear your plans. Travel is so difficult that I rather imagine you will be staying on for the present where you are, but it is hard to visualize any situation on the basis of our meager news. You may have to leave Resht.

These are days when so many are bearing burdens of grief and loneliness that one's own just makes one realize ones common humanity, but how different is the situation for those of us whose trust is in God from that of those who don't know him and to whom death is the end. May God comfort you and keep you strong to do His will in the days of testing ahead.

Yours always with much love,
Margaret

DIFFICULT CHOICES

Personal Report
1942

This year has brought to me the gamut of human experience, in the joys of our new home, the happiness over the birth of our little daughter and then the sadness of the breaking up of our home, with the loss of health and death of husband and father. God was good to us in the short life we had together, and the memories that remain are of happy days spent in service for Christ in home and hospital. The kindness and thoughtful hospitality and loving sympathy of our many friends in our times of need this year have also brought to me a new revelation of the goodness and worth of friendship... Now with the New Year again before us, we can only trust Him in His mercy and wisdom to show the way day by day. While the temptation is great to make the effort to get to America in the fall, for the sake of the health of the little one, because my own conscience would not let me desert the Mission medical work in these difficult times, I shall stay on to do what I can to fill the empty places.

Adelaide K. Frame

Medical Report Resht hospital
1941-1942

Resht Hospital has reached a crisis. It has weathered many a hard storm in 20 years of service to the sick of Resht and its environs, but always with Dr. Frame at the helm. Now with his passing on, we who are left do not want to see it, as a Mission Hospital, flounder and go under unless the will of the Mission as a whole is for such an ending. We would like to see young Dr. Frame come out to Iran as soon as possible to take over in his father's place. Our hope for the future of the hospital lies here.

THE STAFF

This year the hospital was closed for 13 weeks, four weeks in the summer for vacations and nine weeks in December, January, and February due to the illness of Dr. Frame. He returned to work about the middle of February and continued at work until the middle of May, despite increasing fatigue. After a few days of rest at that time, he was able to work only three more days when illness overcame him. Mrs. Frame has carried on part time both before and since his death on June 11th. Mrs.

Frame was also at work from April to mid-October and early December, in Teheran, a new little Frame daughter was born...

SCHOOL OF NURSING

We were proud to have the School of Nursing graduate four more students last October – promising young women who could add much to the community life of any city in Iran. One of the four remained at work in the hospital. Miss Nicholson still has Government permission to conduct the School, and the Department of Education continues to receive our reports and plan for examinations. Last fall three new students were accepted for the Junior class, all of whom are making good progress. There are three members in the senior class.

BABY CLINIC

Many babies were kept or put on the road to health this year through the bi-weekly service of the Well Baby Clinic. It kept its doors open even while the hospital was closed and the average number of babies seen has increased. A significant and important part of the Baby Clinic has been the calling in the homes of the patients which often afford a good opportunity for a bit of helpful evangelistic talk as well as advice and check up on the mother's care of the baby.

STATISTICS

Statistics as such have naturally fallen off this year because the Doctor Weeks were much fewer. But considering the interruptions and curtailments due to health, a goodly volume of work has been carried on. Certainly even after the hospital was closed for nine weeks, there was no lack of patients before the doors the first week it was open. The only trouble came in regulating the numbers to the strength of the doctor.

There are no especially outstanding cases this year, just the steady stream of all manner of ailments, common to any missionary hospital. The bombardment of the town in August and September brought terror to the hearts of the townsfolk, and the inception of many diseases, often startling deductions, are dated to this time of confusion. Numbers fled to the villages, and for several days, weeks, even months afterwards, patients would come in with a fractured arm or wrist saying,

"Fell off a horse while fleeing from the town"

"Malaria and dysentery developed while I was staying in the village"

"My baby was born in a village and the local midwife attended me, hence the illness"

"Fright at the aeroplanes was the beginning of tuberculosis"

We also cared for a number of bomb casualties, mostly infected wounds or fractures. Later in the year the British Army sent in several civilian motor accident cases for us to treat. Fractures and bone cases seemed to have (been) our specialties this year and we are fortunate to possess a Kirschner Traction Pin outfit, which was often in use.

One does not wish to present arguments for keeping the hospital open. All our hospitals are desperately needed in every city where they have given years of service and where the community has come to depend on them for help at crucial times. In the words of one of our young national Christians, "The hospital has been the tangible Evangelistic work of the Resht church – its service in deed and not word alone, for many years."

Respectfully submitted,
Adelaide Kibbe Frame

Personal Report
1942-1943

Marking time rather than marching has seemed to be the undercurrent of my life this past year. We have lived very quietly in our compound in Resht with plenty of work in the hospital, and best of all a wee girl runs down the path, arms out to meet me when I enter the garden gate. Throughout the day are several hours of play and pleasure with her, feeding and caring for her, watching her grow and develop into an active, healthy child. This has been a particular joy for me. Practically all social activities have been put aside, for it has been a problem to keep my time properly balanced between duty to the hospital and duty to the home and baby. It can be done but takes a stable, healthy nervous system, and mine at times has a tendency to let me down. It is in this respect that I seem to be marking time, for the present arrangement should not be considered permanent, but temporary carrying on in an emergency for the duration.

In the meantime, when not being mother and housekeeper, I am doctor and surgeon. For people still will put cabbage leaves on abscesses to cure them, get ruptured appendices, cut by axes or exploding guns, gored by cows, burned because of carelessness, develop tumors and tummy aches, clawed by Mazenderan tigers, have babies normally and abnormally, and a hundred other ailments requiring surgery. And that is how I have been best able to serve the community and our mission cause, backed by all of our faithful, hardworking hospital attendants.

So many patients who come to me, and to hear this is a new experience for me, even the beggars on the street say, "For the sake of your child help me. May God keep her safe for you." Yes, I may be only marking time here this year, but millions of other men and women are marching on. Our prayer is that through them God may be given the opportunity to keep all little children safe in this world!

Respectfully submitted,
Adelaide K. Frame

During the war years the 'Lend-Lease' aid program between America and Russia involved shipping supplies and materials from the Persian Gulf ports in Iran to the Caspian Sea ports and on into Russia. The information written about this time does not include the fact that our home and hospital compound were used as stopover sites during the Americans' visits to the area.

Photo 6.5 Military visiting our home in Resht, 1943

Photo 6.6 Military vehicle in hospital yard, 1943

WAR TIME SHORTAGES

Resht Hospital Report
June 1943

Having heard little or nothing of Resht Hospital since last summer, you may be surprised to learn that we have had a good year in many respects, even though the ways and means of obtaining necessities often are not apparent, for very long ahead.

The death on June 11th (1942) of Dr. J. D. Frame, the founder of and worker in Resht Hospital for the past thirty-seven years, left a great gap in our staff. His sound advice and judgment have often been sorely needed these past months

After a five-week closing and time of consideration, the hospital again opened with Dr. A. K. Frame, the lone American M.D. She has carried the entire surgery and hospital responsibility, conducting the usual three outpatient clinic days each week, the ever enlarging T.B. clinic, fluoroscopies, and pneumothoraces and any night surgery needed... .

In November, Dr. Mohamed Kar, a German-French schooled Christian Iranian, with a German wife and two small children, came from Teheran under a year's contract, to work part time in hospital, especially in the morning outpatient clinic. In the main, this arrangement has worked very well, as he is a quietly energetic man with a true physician's compassion for the sick and needy. Dr. Kar not doing surgery, has been somewhat of a disadvantage, since Dr. Frame's baby is still young enough to require night attention. We had hoped to have someone helping in surgery and taking night calls.

Dr. Kar and his wife are essentially laboratory people and almost immediately they suggested responsibility for this work, keeping on Bahram Chahri whom we have had for the last ten years as an assistant. However, Bahram thought his prestige would be lessened and decided not to remain. Dr. and Mrs. Kar took over the laboratory and equipment the first of January, adding a few supplies, agreeing to do all routine examinations for bed-patients, charging for such tests as Widal, Weil-Felix, and so on. (Wassermans have not yet been started.) All examinations for outpatients are charged for at a reasonable fee, the hospital paying for the free patients, just as it does the drugs for this class of people.

In return the Kars get laboratory rooms with equipment and furniture, light, heat, telephone, cleaning service, some autoclaving and all outside or city work, the income for which hitherto came to the hospital. At present there is no other reliable laboratory in Resht.

SCHOOL OF NURSING

...Resht still maintains a Government recognized school, though the teaching staff has been somewhat depleted. Mrs. Frame has given generously of her few afternoon hours, and Miss Wilder has taught English, Personal Hygiene and Dietetics. Dr. J. D. Frame always took a keen interest in the class work, also Miss Benz helped in many ways. The Iranian nurse, who for years most acceptably taught Anatomy, married and moved to Teheran. Mrs. Kar can teach in four different languages, none of which happen to be Persian. The Government, through the Superintendent of Schools, is still interested and giving examinations to three girls who have completed three full years this coming September.

To enable us to keep up a fair standard of nursing service, we must accept new classes year by year and I feel that this Government connection is worth continuing, hoping that it may be a wedge into a wider field of usefulness later.

...As is true all over Iran, we have paid high for heat. Charcoal averaged about ten times pre-war price. Firewood, for which our hospital is equipped, becomes increasingly expensive and difficult because the Russians, having carts and lorries, can send into the jungle and bring out at fair prices, what they want. On the other hand, we are dependent on what transportation is possible, mostly horses. Just now we are endeavoring to put in about a six month's supply, but can procure very little as yet and that of a smaller variety, quicker burning.

...As this report is being written, we see the effect of the news leaking out that Dr. Frame expects to leave town on her vacation. Many people, especially women, are trying to see her. And so another hospital year draws to a close, a year of some preaching, especially of a Sunday morning in the waiting room, more teaching in many ways and much healing in Christ's name.

Respectfully submitted,
E. D. Nicolson

CRISIS

Resht Hospital Report
June 1944

A patient comes in with curvature of the spine, perhaps it is a general physical weakness in his makeup, possibly from long years at a certain job, or maybe there is actual disease of his vertebrae that is in the links of his backbone.

Resht Hospital, like this patient, has gradually developed a weakness of the backbone. The links which held it together and made it an integrated, efficient, busy institution, bringing healing and health to the sick, are about to collapse.

The sterilizer is completely worn out, the large primus stove for heating it is gone; several special instruments like the cystoscope, necessary for examinations, have broken from constant use; the running water system of the building after 15 or 20 years of use, has collapsed, and flooring is breaking through in places from dampness, the linoleum is worn out and looks untidy; the X-ray machine and tubes are on their last legs and the whole instrument is outmoded and too small. Stoves and heating arrangements will have to be renovated and changed and even the doctor, while decidedly not in a state of collapse, needs a bit of mental, spiritual, perhaps even physical repair work.

All in all we have come to a crisis. We are limping along, not able to stand straight and cannot, until some new strength is put into our backbone. And don't think we haven't tried to patch and nail together and get along without. But one cannot stand upright and look forward, and around and upward, if ones back is humped over.

Resht Hospital has not only had trouble with its backbone because of collapse of equipment and material, but also the vital part of any institution, the very heart of it, is in a weakened state. We refer to our personnel. Dr. A. K. Frame, the American doctor was only supposed to work half time, the other half to be devoted to her baby daughter and home. But sick folk are notorious for using a doctor's free time, so much of that second half was more than likely to be spent in the hospital. We have had no full-time American doctor to put his whole heart and soul into the work as heretofore.

Because of long furlough and delayed return of Miss Benz, Miss Nicholson, our nurse, was forced to do the work of several people. Superintendent of Nurses and of the Nursing School in which she did much of the teaching, matronship of hospital, involving the difficult problem of supplies, and after the departure of our treasurer, (she was married) the keeper of the books. This is too much to expect of any one person, but she has been able to stand up, even do more, carry on under this full load, and is now going to stay on alone so that at least the dispensary and X-ray can be kept going. At the present time, Miss Benz is on her way out and we hope will soon arrive and take over the matronship work.

The National doctor, Dr. Mohamed Kar, on a part-time basis, has been at work every morning of the week in the clinic, thus relieving some of the congestion of patients waiting to consult with a doctor. Likewise has been in the

Baby Clinic for consultation one afternoon and working in our tuberculosis clinic two afternoons each week...

FINANCES

These have been a law into themselves. With the rising prices and consequent rise in the living wage, they have been complicated enough to make any ones backbone weak. We were, of course, forced to increase our fees for tickets, private rooms, operating, etc. and while we have taken in a surprising amount of money, we have likewise paid out amazing amounts for wages, supplies, food, firewood, etc. This year all of our Iranian mission hospitals have had very generous help from the Board, a sum which was used for the mission employees in the form of bonuses and another amount for costlier medicines and drugs. Also the Red Cross has been kind enough to remember our mission hospitals with bandages, some drugs, blankets, and surgical supplies. This has all helped to fill our storerooms and keep our surgery going, as gauze and cotton for instance, to mention just two items, are sold at prohibitive prices in the local bazaar.

NURSING

As usual in the Fall, the senior students, after three years of work and study, took the Government examination and gave good account of themselves. This examination was under the auspices of the local department of education and health. As is often true, the Iranian doctors setting the questions and marking papers, were surprised that the girls could answer so comprehensively. The same young doctors also seemed to enjoy going through the hospital and watching the three students do the practical work which they then graded...

As we have no nurses' home, the girls come from various parts of the city each morning. In winter often they start before it is light to gather at seven o'clock for report of the night nurses and change of shift. It is at this time when we have our devotions, talks, teaching questions about interesting patients, and so on ... A provincial hospital such as Resht must have a Nursing School. Otherwise sufficient and competent nursing is not available.

Respectfully submitted
Adelaide K. Frame

Because of the war in Europe and Asia, my mother and I were not able to leave Iran until June of 1944. Our trip was facilitated by the American government, in exchange for information on the activities of the Russians in the area of Resht. We traveled across North Africa stopping at military air bases, catching whatever plane was going on towards Casablanca. The soldiers we met along the way were lonely for their own homes and children, so that seeing us in this field of war brought them a brief moment of pleasure. My mother told me stories about that trip. In Tripoli, Libya, she and I went out on to the airfield to ask the Italian prisoners of war working there, if they knew when the next plane would be leaving. One of them was so touched to see a young child that he took off his ring and gave it to me. I kept that ring for many years. At another American base along North Africa, possibly Tunisia, she left me in a booth in the cafeteria while getting something for us to eat. When she returned to the booth, it was surrounded by military personnel trying to talk to me. I guess I was totally overwhelmed by it all. Finally on June 8, two days after D-Day, we were able to get on a plane in Casablanca going to America. My mother told me that she felt the military knew more about what was going on in our area than she did, as she was too busy running the hospital alone to be concerned.

Photo 6.7 Adelaide and Margaret arriving in New York, 1944

On her return home the local newspapers published articles about her life in Resht as follows:

WOMAN MEDIC FROM PERSIA RETURNS AFTER EIGHT YEARS

PUBLISHED IN BERKELEY GAZETTE, BERKELEY, CA
JULY 10, 1944

Excitement at Treating Tiger Wounds Nothing to Seeing Daughter with Doll.

Treating tiger wounds of natives was not nearly as exciting for Dr. Adelaide Kibbe Frame, medical missionary to Persia, as seeing her small daughter's joy over her first American doll.

At the home of her parents, Mr. and Mrs. L. H. Kibbe, 33 Eucalyptus Road, Doctor Frame is in the United States after an eight years' absence. For Margaret Frame, 2 1/2 years, Berkeley is a wonderful place. She says so in a mixture of Persian and English as she fondles a collection of dolls and plays with the first real toys she has known.

"In Persia, all she had were homemade toys," her intrepid surgeon-mother explained. "To say she loves her dolls is putting it mildly. She worships them."

Long Service

Her last eight years at Resht on the Caspian Sea, now under Russian control, Doctor Frame added to seven years spent at American Hospitals supported in Persia by the Presbyterian Board of Foreign Missions. The Persian city of 100,000, she said had become a busy war center for transportation by the Allies of material flowing to the Russian armies. Inflation and rationing mark the new

Persian war order, revealed the Berkeleyan, who ran the Resht Hospital alone for two years following the death of Dr. John D. Frame, her missionary husband, in 1942 after 37 years of service in the Near East.

"Food is available but prices are high as wages are up as a result of war activities," Doctor Frame said. "For instance, I paid $6 for a pound of rolled oats! Sugar and rice are rationed despite the fact that Resht is the center for those two commodities and tea. We have our coupons there, too."

Mills, U.C. Graduate

Doctor Frame, graduate of Mills College and of the University of California Medical School and member of a missionary family, which pioneered in that field in China, flew from Teheran to New York with more ease and comfort than she negotiated the wartime trip across the United States, she laughed.

As for that air trip, representing 43 hours flying time over a six-day period, little Miss Frame, en route to the United States to learn about 'American manners' – and toys – was revealed as the sweetheart of the pilots and all the other homesick Americans encountered along the way. "Those boys were so lonely for their own homes and children that seeing a small girl released all their memories and we all had a grand time," Dr. Frame recounted.

As for her own service in Persia, Doctor Frame is modestly quiet. It remained for others to relate that she was the only medic in Resht besides a native Persian, who has now taken charge of her 34-bed hospital, assisted by one nurse.

Tiger wound story

The story of treating tiger wounds, Mrs. Kibbe relates, is one of her favorites concerning the versatility of her daughter's work.

"A wood cutter was attacked by a tiger but manages to grab the animal's tail and swing him off into space while he made his escape," recounts Mrs. Kibbe. "It was five or six days before the native made his way to the hospital and by that time his face was badly infected. But Adelaide pulled him through."

Mrs. Kibbe is greatly amused at her granddaughter's Persian 'jabbering'. She recalls that her own babyhood was similar, only that she spoke Chinese exclusively until she was three, having been born in China, while her father, Dr. Ira M. Condit, blazed the mission trail for others to follow through the years. Doctor Frame plans to remain in Berkeley for a year or longer before once more taking up duties of her Persian post.

BACK FROM IRAN

BY HAL JOHNSON, *OAKLAND TRIBUNE*, AUGUST 1944

It's 100 feet below sea level in Resht on the Caspian Sea and at this time of year this part of perspiring Persia – Iran now – is worse than Washington, D.C., in dog day August, which is a polite way of making the proverbial weather comparison.

In that part of Iran a Berkeley matron has worked for eight years as a medical missionary. She is honest when she says she misses it as much as she often yearned for Berkeley while she was in the semi-tropic city of some 110,000 population and where she and a missionary nurse from Chicago were the only American women. (Only during the last year.)

Since the United States went into wartime production, the rural city has become a transportation center for Allied-made material bound for the Russian armies. Resht knows inflation and rationing. Sugar, rice and tea are rationed. Gasoline is plentiful, but is lack of tires that is keeping the American-made popular price cars off the numerous good roads of Iran. Meat – that is mutton and beef – are plentiful. Rolled oats were selling for the equivalent of $6 a pound when Dr. Kibbe left there.

Yes, Iran has its movies, and audiences, especially in Resht, are extremely active while in theaters. Pictures are shown with a flea obligato and live upholstery keeps film fans squirming more than syncopated melodies or murder mysteries.

Captions are in Russian, Iran(ian), Arabic and French, and the sound, of course, is in English. Technicolor films delight the throngs. Movie operators, not too familiar with the English language or even operating the projectors, speed up the films so that in wedding sequences the bridal parties fairly run down the church aisles. Film kisses are truly facial smacks...

Dr. Frame and daughter, Margaret, left Resht around the first of June and went to Teheran. From there they flew to New York. Flying time was 43 hours in a six-day period... Mother and daughter arrived in New York June 10. They came across country, visiting relatives and friends, including those of her late husband, Dr. John D. Frame. His sister, Miss Margaret Frame, who was a missionary of the Presbyterian Board in Shanghai, was returned home on the last voyage of the S.S. Gripsholm.

...When their daughter was hardly six months old (Dr. John Frame) was stricken with a complication of diseases. You can readily imagine what Dr. Adelaide Kibbe Frame went through. With a youngster who demanded some of her time, despite a native nurse, and a critically ill husband, over whom she worked night and day, she also had to take charge of the 34-bed hospital. There were operations to be performed almost daily, emergency cases, which took her time, and hospital to manage. Miss Ellen Nicholson, a missionary nurse from Chicago, pitched in and helped her. It was a terrific struggle for the two women. Then Dr. John Frame died...

Yes, Resht, foreign as it is, means much to Dr. Adelaide Kibbe Frame, for in the Iran city are fond memories of great joy and deep sorrow, where a heroic woman of medicine became a bride, a mother and a widow all in seventeen months. And little Margaret Frame, playing for the first time with American dolls, which she lovely addresses in the Iran tongue while here on a visit to her Grandpa and Grandma Kibbe, has begun to realize that she had no papa like most of the girls her age.

Serenity Prayer

God grant me the serenity to

Accept things I cannot change,

Courage to change the things I can,

Wisdom to know the difference.

Living one day at a time,

Enjoying one moment at a time,

Accepting hardship as a pathway to peace,

Taking, as Jesus did,

This sinful world as it is,

Not as I would have it,

Trusting that You will make all things right,

If I surrender to Your will,

So that I may be reasonably happy in this life,

And supremely happy with You forever in the next.

Amen.

Reinhold Neibuhr (1943)

CHAPTER 7

Carrying On 1946—1948

After two years in America waiting for the war to end, in the summer of 1946 we started back to Iran and home. My memories of those years are mixed. In order to help me learn English, my mother put me in a nursery school when I was three – I hated it. I was a shy child around other children and had a hard time making friends with these strange American children. My best memories are of my 84-year-old grandmother playing with me and teaching me how to make toasted English muffins in her old stove. One day after sliding down the bannister, I dared her to do it also – which she promptly did! When my mother and grandfather came home, I went running to the door to tell them how Grandmother slid down the bannister. A few days later a very nice housekeeper came to live with us to 'take care of' Grandmother and me. I'm not sure which of us they thought was the more daring! By April of 1946 the Mission Board began the process of sending us back to Iran. My mother would speak to me in Farsi to help me remember the language and prepare for our return.

THE LONG ROAD HOME

FIRST LETTER FROM ADELAIDE FRAME AFTER
SAILING

July 27, 1946
Nearing Gibraltar

Dearest Family,

What a ship! But she does have several excellent points – she's the steadiest I have ever been on (least vibration and rolling) and she's making excellent time, a troopship, the *Marine Carp* – now with 900 passengers aboard! It's terribly crowded – not privacy much and for so many no place to sit on deck – as no deck chairs are provided and no effort made to find anything to sit on. Some have managed to get hold of empty boxes (crates) for stools.

The passengers are a grand mixture – Syrians returning home, Jews to Palestine (many only going on vacation, but planning to stay), Greeks to Piraeus, and many Americans going to Greece for UNRRA, missionaries. One hears many languages spoken and if one could get acquainted with them, no doubt there would be interesting stories. One is a Jew going to Palestine – the only remaining member of his family at all left in Poland, had been in America one week and now going on to Palestine. He has been starved and still wolfs his food.

The three children (English children Mother chaperoned from N.Y.) – well, they're a host in themselves! By the time I have gotten two of the four 'showered' and in bed, and a third on the way to bed, I feel sympathy with a mother who has six! The oldest girl of 12 is a grand child – quite mature and maternal and sweet. She's a big help and takes responsibility for them. The second is a problem child – difficult to manage and doesn't like sister to boss her. The little boy (six) is a normal kid! I think I was a gump to take them on and wouldn't do it again. The ship goes to Haifa first so the children will have to go on to Alexandria alone. Barbara Ann (the oldest of the three children) thinks she can manage.

We have seen no land so far, only one ship, plenty of porpoises playing around, flying fish, and twice the ship has swerved in her course to see what was floating in the water – once it seemed to be a dead whale, and again this morning an abandoned raft! Daily we have fire and boat drill for as they announced, there are still many floating mines!

Sunday morning – July 28

This morning after breakfast we passed the Azores, so my heading 'nearing Gibraltar', was a bit premature! We hope that will be where we are tomorrow early. About nine this morning there was a service up on the sun deck – lovely fresh huge, blue sky and warm sun, blue ocean around us, the peaks of the Azores (Santa Maria) rising up on our port side.

Margaret and two or three other children are playing at my feet, working a puzzle. We have found all of her toys and books most useful and we're grateful to all who contributed. Margaret Frame[14] arranged for someone

14   Margaret Frame, my father's sister who had been in China, was
      waiting for her own clearance to return to her mission work there.
      Later, after her return to China, she was put under house arrest by
      the Communist regime and finally released in 1949.

in the Board Rooms to give us candy and me a book (Dr. Hume's new book on medical missions). The black bag is now full of books and toys!

Yesterday we saw whales cavorting around, standing on their heads and waving their tails in the air, and spouting water. Also an airplane flew over and around us several times, dipping one wing before flying on. That was the extant of excitement for the day! Oh no, three Persian boys appeared, made themselves known and had a good talk with Fishers and all of us – one is with him now. It was good to hear Persian again, though they spoke English well, too.

Saturday morning – Aug. 3

Well, tomorrow, Sunday a.m. we reach Haifa – far quicker than anticipated. We hope to be off for Tiberias and then return Monday to look after our heavy baggage, then Tuesday perhaps on to Persia. So today we pack, write final letters and rejoice that we soon get off! We're tired of it, even though it hasn't been too bad.

Since writing you we had a change in the weather and had a really rocking ship so that many were seasick – I stayed out all I could and didn't have to lean over the rail – but I couldn't eat supper or scarcely any lunch in the dining room. Friends brought out a sandwich and apple which tasted fine on deck. Margaret was fine – so the other children most of the time. The three youngest don't eat any too well, but seem to get along and play happily.

The storm was over the next day and we finally came to Gibraltar Tuesday and passed into the Mediterranean. It was rather hazy (about 6 p.m.) and we couldn't see too clearly but it was very lovely sight – the Golden Gate seems very narrow in comparison! We could see Europe and Africa and the children were thrilled and impressed. We watched both sides for a long time until the light faded. Dolphins were playing about the prow of the ship, to our delight – sometimes three in a row, jumping and diving and having the best time.

For two days we were in sight of land (African shore), lonely mountains and beaches and islands – the mountains reminding us of Iran's rocky, barren peaks. Yesterday we saw nothing, not even a ship. Today Crete is faintly visible. On Thursday lots of ships passed us and from 11:00 a.m. until 8:00 p.m. we were in waters where mines had been heavily laid – we were told to have our life preservers handy. The prow of the ship had been wired with radar arrangements to warn of and repel mines and we were told to keep away from the prow. We saw several battleships and corvettes on guard. Nothing happened and we sail on! All is arranged for the children to go on to Alexandria with a fine missionary couple who go to Sudan (U.P.). Their father cabled a reply to mine. I think they will be happy and can probably spend some time in Haifa if all is peaceful there while the ship is in port for two days.

And now I'm saying goodbye to you all – another leg of the journey is most over and we go on to new countries. My thoughts travel backwards to you.

Adelaide

Photo 7.1 USNS Marine Carp (www.navsource.org)

This trip is one of my earliest complete memories – playing with the children, having a fever and being confined to my bunk, which was the top of three, right under the bulkhead – very claustrophobic. Because Haifa's harbor was mined, we had to disembark outside the harbor and take small boats to the dock. This meant climbing down open steps, attached to the outside of the ship, into a small boat. I remember starting down the steps by myself, as my mother was waiting to have our passports stamped for entry to the area. When about halfway down I stopped and looked back for my mother and recall all the horrified faces looking down at me, a four-and-a-half-year-old going down those steps alone. I was very proud of what I was doing. It was a great adventure. I think the passport official was afraid to move as his hand seemed to be frozen in midair. The poor man helping passengers into the boat at the bottom just about had a heart attack when he saw me waiting my turn to be helped in.

I remember swimming in the Sea of Galilee and the long bus trip across the desert. We stopped once at a *caravanserai* in the middle of the night where I had hot milk to drink. Knowing the tendency for baggage to disappear in transit, my mother would climb up on the top of the bus after each stop to make sure it was still all there.

Photo 7.2 Checking on baggage

Hamadan, Iran
August 16, 1946

Dear Ones all:

We entered the land of Persia on Aug. 13th, just three weeks and a day after leaving N.Y. – excellent time. Here we are now in Hamadan, where it is cool and delightfully restful – arriving last evening around 7:30. We leave Monday morning, the 19th for Tehran – one more stop before our final one. Margaret keeps asking, "Is this where we are going to live? I want to go where Sandy (my dog) is right now!"

Our trip has really been quite successful and not too hard – especially now that it is nearly over and we consider it in retrospect. None of us have been ill, we have had no serious delays or losses or real trouble and count it a good journey, so far.

I believe my last letter was mailed in Haifa after landing there – less than two weeks ago – though it seems a *long* time. (We have gone through so many countries and traveled in so many different conveyances.) To return to the events of the trip up to Hamadan – we spent part of one very hot day there (Haifa), working over our baggage and freight, getting it in the shape to send overland to Teheran.

That afternoon we decided to take just a few of our bags and go over to Tiberias by bus on the Sea of Galilee – an interesting ride across Palestine through Nazareth (a busy little town on a hillside) and Cana, and down to the lake – so blue, surrounded by the barren, wrinkled hills – and hot, too. We had comfortable (as good as can be expected there) rooms in a hotel quite close to the Lake, their dining room and bathing place separate, and down a road and steps to the shore. We stayed two nights and a day there, washing clothes and hair, writing cards, swimming in the Lake (Margie just loves the water), sleeping. Miriam Mouray, a new teacher going to Teheran, went to Jerusalem and returned Wednesday to join us for Damascus. That night more swimming and a boat ride (only a short one, as the police refused permission to be on the Lake after dark.)

The next morning we were up at six to catch the 7:00 a.m. bus back to Haifa to get our Special bus (Arab) on to Damascus. Later we discovered to our chagrin that this bus went right through Tiberias and we could have picked it up there. It is about 300 miles to Damascus from Haifa and 500 from Damascus to Baghdad. We enjoyed the climb up from Lake Galilee, crossing the Jordan far up – caught glimpses of the Lake and valley for a long time – fine views of Mount Hermon with only a little snow. The various customs, passports, and so on took so much time that it was 6:00 p.m. before we reached Damascus. Here the air was cooler and drier than humid Palestine. We stayed at the Orient Palace Hotel – best in town and quite elegant in some ways, though the next morning Margaret seemed to have some 'bites' – pretty definitely of the bedbug variety! At noon we were at the Nairn Depot to board our stage – this time the deluxe one, (huge big aluminum, painted blue with airtight windows and air conditioned so that no dust entered and we stayed cool and comfortable). They served tea, dinner, ice water for drinking and even a lavatory and washbasin – blankets for our reclining chairs. So we rode in luxury over the desert, watched the great swirls of reddish dust blot out the light at times, saw the sunset red and gold, the moon rise, and on we went with the minimum of stops. Rutbeh Wells, where we used to stop, is all changed – an Arab village now, and the 'hotel' destroyed in bombing raids. We slept in our reclining chairs, though I'm not so good at that. The bus was not full by about eight or ten passengers, going that way, but will be booked up for weeks going the other direction, this time of year.

We arrived in Baghdad about 9:00 a.m. – 21 hours or little less. Mr. Lampard met us, helped us through customs and took us to the Y.M.C.A. where we were cordially welcomed and made 'comfortable', this advisedly, because it was so hot – at least seemed so to us. We stayed until Monday evening – did errands in the Bazaar, had lunch at the American Legation, and then at

8:00 p.m. took the night train to Khanaquin. It was fine to be on that little old train, even though hot. We four gals were together in one first class compartment, and the two Fishers in another. There were two electric fans going in each compartment and with the breeze of traveling in the night, we were able to keep cool enough to really sleep and rest some in our berths. I thought the train less bumpy and jerky than ones in U.S., though of course there were no curves – just a straight line!

Yes, we are in our own house – since yesterday morning early, and so glad to be here. So far, I have seen only a few people – all quite cordial. I have been busy, of course, trying to get settled – quite a job in a house this size. But it's fine to be here and I do love this house and yard. Margie feels strange and rather lost, I fear, and as she can't speak the language, perhaps she is a bit homesick for you all in California. She asks me several times a day what I think Grandma or Grandpa or Ginny are doing. A fine swing was put up for her in the garden, and a set of parallel bars has been ordered for her pleasure! Also there are at least two nice little girls (both Armenian) in town and perhaps later an English child with whom she can play. Also I have a cook – some 10 or 12 years ago was cook for the Shedds and Hancocks here in Resht – and seems to know our ways pretty well. I am taking him on and hope he will turn out to be a good cook. Gertrude tried him out beforehand to get him started. She also had the house cleaned and as ready as she could without going into my storeroom much. Now I'm getting out all the little things, fixing closets, and so on. She even put up tomatoes for me and jams and jellies, and I've fruit of Ellen's so we're off to a good start. Living is still *high*.

The trip from the border on up into Persia was not so eventful. The Hamadan trip to Resht was a headache. Our 'good' car broke down – i.e. three punctures, one a complete blowout, laid us up, so we transferred to a truck that finally came along and arrived at 5:00 a.m., instead of 6:00 p.m. the night before! But here we are! So thankful for a safe journey and good health for us both.

Sandy was here to greet Margaret and she calls him 'Sandy boy' in a very honey voice. Today he played in the garden with us, running after a stick we threw, just as I had told her he would do, and had done when she was a baby. That tickled her so – that and her swing. I hope I can get these parallel bars made right. The question of finding someone to look after her is not settled as yet. Servants' wages are so high I shall have to cut down all I can. But I need time to work out a plan that is best.

So far I've not mentioned the hospital. I haven't been over there yet – too busy trying to get settled at home. Of course, the building is closed up and there's not much to see – rather discouraging. After I get the ménage here running fairly smoothly, then I'll begin over there where there is also plenty to do.

I'm afraid I'm too sleepy to write more. Bed, even under a mosquito net, sounds quite delightful. I do miss having running hot water! Think Margaret is learning about only drinking boiled water and eating only washed fruit.

A big hug and a kiss from us both.
Adelaide

Photo 7.3 Our home in Resht and Sandy

BACK AT WORK

EXTRACT OF A LETTER OF NOVEMBER 17, 1946
DR. ADELAIDE FRAME

It's cold this morning although the sun is shining. We walk down to Persian Church, getting home in time for dinner at noon. This afternoon after I get Margaret to sleep, I must go to the home of my latest baby case to see how she is. In some respects I rather enjoy this going to the house for deliveries. It is interesting to be in on their home life, to become better acquainted with them. That part I enjoy thoroughly. But it does take a lot of time and being away from home and Margaret when I am supposed to be with her. I try to make the after calls when she is asleep or in the morning when she is with her teacher. This present case is an old friend – her family and her husband brought out a little toy puzzle John had given him when a little boy. They are very friendly and thoughtful and trust me implicitly as only Persians could do! I just finished another baby case of about the same type. These friends happen to be of the wealthy class.

We are really busy now getting the hospital into shape – repairing the linoleum where torn and worn with strips of copper, painting doors and cupboards – only where needed most – putting on new oil cloth, and so on. Gertrude is very busy cleaning, scrubbing (that is the cleaning women do that under *her* supervision), airing mattresses and pillows, making new curtains for screens and windows and so on. She is a wonderful help as matron and loves to do it, too. We have decided to fix up one private room especially attractively and will try to keep it so. This room we will try to keep nice, charge more for it and we feel sure some of our clientele will very much appreciate it and be willing to pay for it. Our other *private* rooms we are going to try to fix up too although not quite to this extent. I rather think it would be appropriate to let the money the women of the church gave me as a 'purse' that day at the Association Meeting pay for fixing up this room. Then I shall write them from time to time about the patients who occupy it.

The new electric pump has not yet arrived from Tehran – it's annoying to have to use pitchers of water and have it poured in order to wash one's hands! And we still have not enough nurses lined up to begin work – that is a serious problem. The storerooms are being rebuilt and enlarged.

Today has been really hot for there has been one of those freakish hot winds blowing. I think I told you how they often come in cold weather and dry everything up and warm you through – then usually a cold spell of rain and occasionally snow follows. It has been cold but today was so hot Margaret put on a sun suit! Resht does have the queerest climate. There is no good explanation for these hot winds – a meteorologist or some such professor might find them an interesting study – do they come from the Sahara or where?

Exchange rate is high now – 48 *reals* to the dollar this month, which helps some – although the high cost of living is terrific still and here in Resht is much worse than in some of the other provincial towns. Sugar is 83¢ a pound and lump sugar in cones is about $1.04 per pound in the local bazaar. This is very hard on the poor folk. I hope there will be sugar rations given out at a lower rate soon for them. The whole thing is a terrible graft.

April 7, 1947

Dear Family,

Did you have a Happy Easter Day? Margaret and I got up for our 6:00 a.m. sunrise service at the church – followed by breakfast together – Persian style (except for fruit, stewed apricots) bread, cheese, greens, tea and sugar, and hard-boiled eggs. It was pleasant to eat together. Then Margaret and I went home where she enjoyed hunting Easter eggs – which we had colored, and I enjoyed a cup of coffee. Next came her Sunday School lesson, then the hospital (vice versa, I guess), then 11:00 church, dinner, Margaret's nap while I rested, and then out calling – five calls on friends – especially

Armenians and one Jewish family for their Passover. They (the Jewish family) serve just tea, unleavened bread, nuts and fruit – the Armenians heavy cakes and candy as well. We felt stuffed by nighttime and ready for bed. Margaret drank considerable tea of which she is very fond!

Then in regard to the auto[15], Mr. Payne wrote from Tehran that Chevrolets just aren't to be had now. Willy's station wagons are something like $3500 in Tehran! Station wagons are getting popular here – that is, you see them occasionally! And all of our stations want one as station property – some day! I believe I will pay the extra cost and ask for one if it's possible.

The hospital is fairly busy right now – was so all day – ending with a major operation at 5:00 p.m. – the patient had a twisted abdominal cept, turning black. All is well so far and tomorrow she ought to be quite comfortable as it was quite an easy operation. The other day we had a very sick young man who had a neglected ruptured appendix 40 days before – he had a large abscess which we opened from his right flank, near the back, not in his abdomen and he is fine too. He may have to have his abdominal operation later. Another young man had a bad osteomyelitis of his leg which is healing marvelously quick with the help of penicillin. Another a ruptured appendix for days with a localized abscess and he is now draining from his intestines which I will have to fix up soon, and plenty of malaria, TB, typhoid, babies, aches and pains and operations of various kinds!

---

15   My mother was trying to buy an auto for her and the mission's use. Eventually the decision was made to order one from America and have it shipped out.

I try to live on my income out here, but just now I am not getting the finally correct amount as the Board Offices made a mistake last fall and have not rectified it yet, up to date. Also our salary here in Resht has been upped a little as Resht prices are higher than any other places in Iran.

Margaret is happy and 'busy' these days. She loves to run over to her Aunt Gertrude's house and suggest she stay for a meal! Her Aunt Gertrude is usually quite thrilled to have her come. She thinks Margaret is pretty fine and the feeling is mutual.

And now it's bedtime – big hug and kiss from each of you from us both.

Adelaide

FULFILLING WORK

Mission report 1947

"Mama, why did we come back to Iran? Why aren't you like other mamas? Don't go to the hospital today, stay home and play with me. I love you clear up to the sky and down to the earth."

When I hear these words as Margaret and I walk down to the front gate in the morning with breakfast over and the day's routine begun, well may I ask myself, "Why did I come back?" Simply the answer is, "My work is here." But it is far more complex than that for most of us; the drawing power of missionary life and work once begun is a strong force that pulls harder as the years go by. Maybe we all are 'peculiar'. Who knows, but once out here we at least have satisfying work to do and plenty of it. And more important even is the privilege of knowing we are actively trying to fulfill the pledge of fealty made to our Lord when we first decide on full time service to Him.

Margaret (then aged four-and-a-half) and I returned to Resht in August 1946 after two years at home in Berkeley, California. That irresistible drawing power pulled us back to try to pick up the threads where they had been broken, and to carry on the tradition of the American Hospital in Resht as best we could. In the fall Margaret was thrilled to be in a weekly kindergarten class of some six or seven children, which Mrs. Browning had throughout the year. Then she has had two little playmates who have made life happier for her, and of course once she learned Persian she felt as though this really was home. She loves people and going visiting is one of her greatest pleasures though I often doubt if it is that for those she visits as she is decidedly a conversationalist. She is looking forward eagerly to the time when she can go to school in Teheran. This fall we shall make some arrangements whereby I can be metamorphosed into 'teacher' for two hours each morning.

It cannot be denied that I do ask myself at times, "Why did I ever come back? Why should I think I could carry on two jobs?" I often fearfully wonder which may be suffering the most, the child or the hospital. Certainly those in the station (and national friends too) have done all they could to be kind and thoughtful of Margaret, which has helped so much to keep her happy and content, to make the difficult times smoother and to restore balance if there were tensions and complications.

I am indeed grateful to be here again, glad to have useful work to do, and can also rejoice to watch the growth and development of the little child in the home.

Respectfully submitted,
Adelaide K. Frame

MORE RESPONSIBILITIES

Resht
September 29, 1947

Dear Family all,

It certainly is a joy to have letters from the home folk and the more the better, and the happier and more settled we feel. Yes, my furlough and its extension of one year did a great deal for me and for Margaret and we loved being with you. It was a difficult decision to make to leave you again and return. I often wonder if I should have done it. But here I am and we hope doing service good for those who need medical help.

Since August 4th I have been home only 10 days! As I wrote you about Sept. 6th, on the 11th we left (Gertrude, Don Wallace, Lynn Browning and I) in a car for Hamadan and the Annual Meeting of our mission. The first big one with several delegates from each Station since 1941 in Tabriz – I went with John then. There were 40 of us there counting the Hamadan folk and some were wives, not all delegates. Our mission was down to about 35 or less, now we have 65, at the peak in the

1930s we had 110. The fellowship and good fun were of course a great treat especially to those of us who come from small station of six or seven, and only three or four other British or Americans. The meetings began with a three-day Evangelistic conference, which was splendid – a real inspiration and help to each one of us. After this conference ended the Annual Meeting business began by breaking up into committees, meeting together again each a.m. for devotions and for any business a committee had for discussion and recommendation. I was elected chairman of the medical committee which had to consider various actions, placement or changes of personnel, policy etc. Also, was on the finance committee, which was difficult for me as 'finance' (good old arithmetic!), was never my strong point and I'm not station treasurer as nearly all were. But I did my best and began to see light a little towards the end – appropriations, estimates, and so on, ever our dreams at night. One really works at Annual Meeting both early and late. We had one night for fun together – good stunts, funny songs, and so on. There were some fine singers in the crowd – and the music and hymns together were a joy. We had so much business that it took over two weeks to finish so that finally on the 26th we broke up and went our several ways home. For breakfast that morning Art Muller carried in a big bowl of hot cereal with a lighted candle on it and placed it before me as they sang 'happy birthday'! (Adelaide's 46th) We had to leave right after breakfast to get our bus – ten of us going to Tehran that day in a big bus. When we stopped for lunch we ate together and when they reached the fruit stage a lovely big box of candy with a card signed by all was presented to me along with 'Happy Birthday to you'. And that night in Teheran others came around and said Happy Birthday. And so my birthday was strung out with presents from Gertrude and Elizabeth Reynolds, and when I reached home on the 27th Eunice Baber (missionary and head nurse at the hospital) and Margaret gave me presents too! It's fine to have a birthday as you travel!

Margaret had a little cold and had fever one day and one stomach upset otherwise had been fine and happy with Miss Baber. Guess she was glad to have me back though. Remarked today she thought she was going to have a good mama who would let her do everything she wanted and now I wouldn't! Today she started in 'school' with Edna Browning as teacher – using her Calvert[16] course. A fine arrangement (at least I hope it will be) has been made to have a little British girl whose father is in the Bank, Ann Sinclair, have lessons with Margaret. The competition will be helpful. Ann is six.

You will be interested to know Annual Meeting has decided to send Margaret and me to Tehran and Dr. Hoffman here to Resht when he returns in January. I am to take care of the Missionary force there (they have been *very* anxious to have one of our doctors there in that big station – as you know Teheran Hospital is closed until we have *more* doctors) and to let Margaret go to school, to the Community School! We cabled Dr. Hoffman and he replied he was willing to try it – it is only a temporary arrangement for us both as he will be needed in Meshed after two years when Dr. Cochran, who is there now, will probably go to Tehran to open up the hospital there. And

16 Calvert School is homeschooling curricula used by families living both abroad and in many states. Courses are approved by the Maryland State Department of Education

Margaret will be old enough to stay alone in Tehran then. While I truly hate to leave Resht and the work here it will perhaps be better all around for the next two years. Hope I can be of service in Tehran to the missionaries and also work in some of the big clinics they have there (Baby Clinics and prenatal). I don't look forward to packing up and moving, nor do I particularly like living in big, busy Tehran. I like the provinces better. Guess I can stand it for two years. I will be doubly glad to have the car there.

And now *lots* of love to each one from,

Adelaide

A WELCOME VISITOR

Sunday Afternoon
October 12, 1947

Dearest Mother and Father,

It is a rainy Sunday evening and damp and rather cold – at least we have an open fire burning on the hearth tonight and it is cozy and cheery. Margaret is fast asleep though it is just 7:00 p.m.. She still wakes up early and though she had a rest this afternoon, no sleep, so was quite tired by dark. We ate supper up here in the living room tonight around my little gateleg table. Elizabeth Reynolds is here visiting me – her vacation for rest and recreation.

I was pretty busy in the hospital last week and didn't have much time at home with her. Still we have done a few things together. One was going to Pahlavi to the beach, Miss Baber went along and Margie, of course.

We had a grand time – Margie went in swimming a little, though we big folk all thought it too cold for more than paddling our toes. But the sun came out warm and pleasant. We watched them catching fish in a very large net (over 200 yards long), crews of men hauling the two ends in by hand. We picked up shells, drank tea and ate cookies and candy and played in the sand. All made possible because Elizabeth rented a car for the afternoon on her vacation money! Someday maybe I will have that car of my own.

Yesterday afternoon we went through the local jute mill, which I had never seen, and found it quite interesting – more so than I had expected. The man in charge (a Scotsman) used to run one in Calcutta – very large one. This one only has 80 looms but seemed good sized to us. They have their own generator for the electric power, too. The man in the machine shop and power plant recognized me and asked if Margaret were Dr. Frame's child. He said every night he remembered Dr. Frame with gratitude for he had saved his left arm for him when it had been injured years ago. Practically daily I hear such tributes of gratitude and respect for John's memory in the city and probably would too were I to travel in the villages.

In our Annual Meeting we were presented with an Evangelistic program which included ideas for advance of our work in many lines, all of course on the evangelistic basis. This we hope to carry out in faith that the funds will be found. For instance here in Resht we asked for funds for an ambulance – said ambulance to be fitted up for medical/evangelistic trips to the villages and small town around about – for dispensary work, minor operations, and examinations, a small electric generator so pictures could be shown, etc. We think this would be a grand thing – already done in India but never tried here just that way. I would like to do that but a second doctor would be needed to care for the hospital while one spent the day or longer in the outfield. We hope it will be possible soon.

Margaret loves her schoolwork. She started off on the 29th with her little school mate Ann Sinclair. Ann's father takes them both in the car. Margaret walks up the street a long block to the gas pump on the corner, by herself (one day she reported some little school girls touched her cheek and face. I asked her what she said to them. She said she really didn't pay any attention she was "in such a brown study". We had read that in a Thornton W. Burgess book and she seems to love to use that expression.) Mrs. Browning teaches the two little girls their reading, writing and 'rithmatic (literally) and I'm supposed to teach General Deformation like looking at pictures, learning poems, and so forth. Have fallen down this past week on my part. Mrs. Browning reports Margaret is making fine progress. They seem to get along very happily together and the competition is a help I'm sure.

And now I must run over to the hospital for a few minutes.

Dearest love as always,
Adelaide

Photo 7.4 Elizabeth Reynolds at the Caspian Sea

DAILY LIFE

Thanksgiving Night, 1947

Dearest Family,

It's all right to be with friends as good as these are out here on these special holidays, but one still longs for one's own family circle!

This morning Margaret did not have school but stayed at home with her 'teacher' (she calls her girl that) who brought her little sister aged four to play. I went to the hospital as usual and had clinic – got home at 12:45 p.m. – in time to get myself and Margaret dressed for 1:30 p.m. dinner at Gertrude's home. We had a very bounteous meal – goose and many trimmings –

so much so that she has asked us all over there tomorrow to help eat up the leftovers. After the meal some of us took a walk up the avenue to recover. Then Eunice and I went to a short medical meeting to which we had been asked – beginning of some lectures on hygiene and public health for the public, back home to read to Margaret and put her to bed early as she was tired. Now I have the evening before me and nothing special to do! Must go to the hospital for rounds and then guess I'll read a bit.

Nov. 28th

Last eve I went over to the hospital and found a woman patient whom I had seen earlier in the evening needed an emergency appendectomy. So we operated then and there, found a 'nice' red hot appendix and were glad we had done it. Before we finished two men were brought in who had been in an auto accident – not seriously hurt but needed examining. So went Thanksgiving night. Today we had more surgery – first a tedious operation but one which I hope will turn out well – may or may not. A child of four had burned his hand seven months previously – was out in a village where he did not get proper attention so that all fingers on one hand were contracted down and adherent to the palm. We put on skin grafts and will wait results whether they take or not. Before we finished that, they brought in a young boy with pain in the upper left side of his abdomen – still don't know just what his diagnosis is. But before we could go eat lunch (leftovers with Gertrude) we opened up a huge abscess of the back, around the kidney, on a woman who had been suffering with it for ten days – in a village. How they stand the pain and suffering that they do we can't understand! I saw in the clinic this morning the boy I may have told you about some month ago – he had been bitten by a snake, probably not too bad – the treatment had been worse – tourniquet left on for days, not just hours, so his toes and front part of foot were black and had to be amputated. We used skin grafts on him, which took well – he still had a few raw spots on his upper leg but most were healed and he gets around with a cane. He is a bright sort. We'd like to have an ambulance for trips to the villages that could continue medical and evangelistic work. We have asked for one on the new Evangelistic program which our Annual Meeting put out this year.

Mr. Payne has not let me know yet whether the car has left Bombay – I surely hope to hear the date soon. In fact I'm daring to contemplate on the pleasure it would be to have the car here by Christmas. I could go up to Teheran to get it (he plans to have it shipped straight up to T – boxed) and bring the Browning children down with me for their X-mas holidays. Then we'd really have a merry Christmas. There have been some beautiful, warm, sunny almost spring like days the past two weeks when we longed for a car to get out a little! It's raining this evening and is cold again. Today I had two trees cut down in the yard – shall miss them but think it better this way – nothing would grow well under one. I planted two new eucalyptus trees along the front path which will be reminders of California – if they grow. And so again goodnight and lots of love and a Merry Christmas and Happy New Year to all, (and a big Christmas hug and kiss from us both)

Adelaide

P.S. Margaret is so excited about her birthday – is counting days regularly and correctly! The big doll is ready except for one dress. The bought one was too small and I will have to have another one made. I am going to fix her up a sewing basket. I think she will be just about overcome by the doll from Grandma. She wants a doll more than anything else.

December 11, 1947

Dear Mother and Father,

Just two weeks from tonight Christmas Day will be nearly over – as usual I cannot realize it is that close and am not ready for it. Tonight I have been writing Christmas cards for Persia friends and I find I am now out of them completely. I am wondering if you could still find them in the stores by the time you get this. It is surprising what can be found in the stores here now and Tehran undoubtedly has even more. I may someday not need to ask you to buy me more things.

Today winter is really upon us, a cold wind is blowing and it is raining hard. Some say it may snow soon. My new kerosene burning army stove (no wick, but oil drips from a carburetor) is doing fine tonight and gives the room a lovely warmth, needs no coaxing or blowing or replenishing while burning. Of course we have to buy kerosene and keep the tank filled but on the whole they are very satisfactory, clean and easy.

In March 1948 my grandmother died and my mother decided to resign from mission work to take care of her father and spend more time as a parent. The strain of trying to run the hospital alone, and responsibilities of motherhood, were becoming too much for her. But that wasn't the end of our life in Resht.

The Rose and the Clay

By the hand of a friend in bath one day

There was given to me some perfumed clay,

"O! musk or ambergris," I said,

"Your ravishing perfume has turned my head!"

It said, "I was naught but worthless clay

Till I sat by the side of a rose one day;

My companion's fragrance affected me;

Otherwise I'm the clay I used to be."

Sa'adi (1184-1291)
Translated by S. J. Jordan

CHAPTER 8

A Happy Return 1950—1953

After we left Iran in June of 1948, Rolla and Helen Hoffman were assigned to Resht to keep the hospital going. Dr. Hoffman had gone out to Iran in 1915 spending most of his years in Meshed, with a brief time in Teheran. In fact he was the doctor in attendance when I was born there. My mother had known Rolla and Helen Hoffman from the very beginning of her time as a doctor in Meshed, and they had always been close friends. In 1949 Helen Hoffman died in Resht after a battle with cancer.

Between 1948 and 1950 we settled into my grandfather's home, with my mother working as a doctor in the Oakland, California, public schools. I started the second grade in a regular classroom after being home schooled in Iran. The Calvert courses that we used taught script right from the beginning, so I never learned to print. One of the difficulties, as any child who has had to transfer schools frequently can tell, is being either ahead or behind the curriculum in the new school. In my new school students in the second grade hadn't learned script yet. As I had never learned to print, I wrote my lessons in script. One day early on, the teacher called me to the front of the classroom and accused me of showing off for writing in script rather than printing. I was mortified and went home in tears. My mother came into school the next day and explained I had been home schooled in Iran and never learned to print. The teacher took great delight in teaching me to print so I would be like everyone else. I adjusted and made a few friends, but always missed Iran and our life there. I was still 'different'.

In the early months of 1950 Rolla Hoffman asked my mother to marry him and return to Iran. I knew she had greatly missed being a missionary and the medical work she had been doing in Iran, although taking care of her father was important to her. My grandfather encouraged her to go back to Iran. Arrangements were made for my cousin and his family to move in with my grandfather when we left. I remember our cook and housekeeper said she wouldn't let me go back until I weighed 50 pounds, so I stuffed myself every meal and got on the scales daily to see how close I was – 48 pounds was the best I could do.

Photo 8.1 Adelaide and Margie 1950

In April of 1950 we returned. Arrangements had been made in Teheran for me to stay with a family as a 'boarding' student for the rest of third grade. As previously noted, my mother had mentioned in letters how much I was looking forward to going to school in Teheran like the other missionary children. The reality was much different. We returned to Iran, my mother was married, and I was left in Teheran for school, all within a week. Over the next three years, Ann Wild, whose parents were English missionaries in Southern Iran, and I lived with four different families. Even though it is a home environment, there are new rules and habits to learn each time. As nice and caring as the families were, it is still not how we did things at 'home'.

Photo 8.2 Wedding party – April 21, 1950

MEETING THE FAMILIAR

Personal Report
June 30, 1950

Little did I think when I said goodbye to *khaki* (khaki colored) Iran as our plane rose over Teheran's dusty plain in June 1948, that in little less than two years we would be descending from the skies over that same plain. Yet how fortunate it is God has so ordained life that we cannot foresee the future. And so, Margaret and I came back to Persia. There followed four busy days of seeing many friends, of making plans for the wedding and trip, of enrolling Margaret in the Community School and installing her in the Bucher's hospitable home for the last six weeks of the term. Then on the afternoon of April 21st, Dr. Rolla E. Hoffman and I were married at a simple service in Miss Doolittle's home with only our missionary friends present, as we wished it to be a small affair. A lovely tea followed contributed by the Teheran housewives. The next 10 days or so we spent in Isfahan and Shiraz visiting with friends in the Anglican Missions in those two cities, seeing Persian friends as well, and spending a memorable day in ancient Persepolis, before flying back to Teheran and driving down to Resht. We are so grateful to all of our friends everywhere for the many letters, telegrams, gifts and other expressions of kindness and love which have come to us.

The first few weeks after our return to Resht were spent in getting the house in order, the ménage running more or less smoothly, greeting old friends and in finding ourselves. Gradually I began some work in the hospital, and find that it is good to get my hand in again. I see quite a number of familiar faces as the days pass in the clinic work – about two hours daily in the clinic, assisting irregularly in surgery or doing a few operations myself, and the weekly visit to the Baby Clinic. As I see anew this small hospital, compact, crowded to the bursting point, busy all the time, yet rendering to the sick the best service that it possibly can, I am made aware, because of the inadequacy of the plant, of the struggle it takes to keep from letting a feeling of complete frustration overcome the one running it. Sunday mornings, between our pancake breakfasts and church, I have been attending medical rounds that I may keep in touch with the patients in the hospital. In the two months we have been here, we have also had the enjoyment of sharing our home and nice garden with several groups of guests as they have come to Resht.

The other day as I was walking in the bazaar in the rain, two portly, dignified *mullahs* in dark cloaks and large white turbans were walking in front of me. Suddenly they stopped, turned around and said, "Dr. Kibbe, I believe." Then they urged me to give special attention to a sick relative being treated in the clinic. A little farther along a ragged boy grinned up at me, one of the youngsters under treatment for favus, his head now bald as a doorknob. And finally, when one of my old beggar friends *salaamed* and looked hopefully at me, I knew I was indeed back in Iran. And with that realization came the feeling that here is where I belong. Surely the Lord had prepared the way for our return to Iran, the arrangements at home in California left with a happy solution, the long trip made in safety and the plans for the wedding and the trip all working out so beautifully. This makes me feel that perhaps He does have work for me to do here in Persia, and naturally much will be required of me.

Adelaide K. Hoffman

September 20, 1950

Dear Friends,

Most of you received the announcement of our marriage, on April 21st. Now, Adelaide relieves me in the clinic about half of each forenoon, while I become Roentgenologist. Our new Picker 'Century' X-ray machine is the only one in this whole province, and is very useful to outside doctors as well as to us in dealing with hospital patients. In fact, our 'Lightening', or electric, machine appeals to the public as something truly magical; and a goodly proportion of clinic patients come to us saying, "I want to sit under the Lightening machine," and it matters little what their trouble may be. We have set the charges at low figures, and many poor are attended free. Such cases as those with needles in hands or feet, fractures and dislocations, are usually simple, but impressive. One woman came limping and groaning, saying she had a needle in her foot. When X-ray examinations failed to find any needle, and she was told there was none, she brightened up at once, and went away without any limp! We find much tuberculosis, and it is distressing to realize that there is no sanatorium to which they can go, except the small one near Teheran, where more than half the patients are from the Resht region.

What kind of patients do we see in our little dispensary five forenoons each week? Well about half are the very poor, and they pay nothing. Most villagers and poorer city folk harbor intestinal worms – often two or three kinds of them. Malaria is terribly common, and often very severe; but now we hope it is going to decrease, since there has been a lot of spraying with DDT in this region, under the 'Seven Year Plan'. There is lots of tuberculosis, of lungs, bones, lymph nodes. We are considered specialists in favus and ringworm of the scalp, and many come asking for the 'lightening' or electric medicine – thallium acetate, which makes the hair fall out. Practically all are much improved, and perhaps a third are cured entirely. We have half a dozen patients with Hansen's Disease (leprosy) under regular treatment with diasone tablets kindly supplied by the American Leprosy Mission. Then we have a goodly number of the well-to-do; on two days each week we see pay patients only.

Now many friends will want to know of our relations with the Russians. Well, we just have no relations with them, except that we see a Russian patient now and then. Their hospitals have been closed in Resht, Tabriz and Meshed; the one in Teheran continues, a center of propaganda. If the Russians come in, well, we shall find ourselves suddenly cut off from the outside world, no doubt. Meanwhile, we keep on with the job.

The little church in Resht has its first Iranian pastor this year, Reverend Faizullah Larudy, who has just returned from America after two years of study in Princeton Seminary. He is a native of Resht, has a rare understanding of both the Iranian and American points of view, and is a fluent speaker in both Persian and English, in addition to knowing the local Geelacky dialect, which is too much for us Americans. He is carrying on research work in the field of Hospital Evangelism, the management of clamoring crowds in the dispensary, the question of whom to see and whom to turn away when more folk come than we can handle, and guiding the hospital employees in the use of their time and the improvement of their talents.

Recently a poor woman fell and broke her arm, which had to be in a cast a couple of months, during which time she and her children were going hungry, as her daily wages stopped. A boy from a wealthy family also had a fall, and came into the hospital for a few days. Mr. Larudy so effectively presented the plight of the poor woman to the boy's mother that she immediately offered to support the poor woman during her incapacity. A wealthy Iranian has a fund which was entrusted to him by a friend at his death, and he is using it to meet the expenses of various poor folk as they come into our hospital. There are great possibilities connected with this Christian hospital, working in a Moslem community, and it is a great privilege to have a hand in it.

Yours sincerely,
Adelaide and Rolla Hoffman

Photo 8.3 Playing backgammon with Persian friends

COMPARTMENTS OF LIFE

Personal Report
June 1951

This report year my responsibilities may be divided into three compartments of home, church and hospital. In the home came the family vacation last summer for most of the hot month of August – three weeks in Hamadan and Teheran made a fine change for us all, the only hardship for me was a painful knee which kept me from much walking or exercise for several months. In mid-September Margie went up to Teheran for the fall school term, and during the year she came home for Christmas, spring and, now, the summer holidays, which meant several trips for us back and forth. She will be in the fifth grade at Community School.

We have had the pleasure of entertaining quite a number of guests, both for meals and as houseguests. When the weather is right, we enjoy a drive to Pahlavi for a swim in the Caspian (Sea) as much as the guests seem to. Our living room in the winter is a good-sized, cheerful room with the afternoon sun; in summer we move outdoors onto the big, upstairs, screened-in porch, one of the choice things about this old house. This compartment of home life gives us special opportunities of fellowship and sharing the privileges of our home with others.

In the hospital, I seem to have developed a triple personality by force of circumstances. First, with the retirement of Miss Benz last winter, I have had to take over some of her duties. We have been able to work in an efficient and reliable Iranian woman for much of the work, though I take the daily kitchen accounts with the cook, have some of the supervision with her of the laundry, sewing and mending, and minor repairs and cleaning of the hospital. Then with the departure of our substitute American nurse, Miss Harvey, the end of last month, and until the return of Miss Degner, I have become a nurse to the extent of giving out nursing supplies from the storeroom and acting as final referee for various problems among the nurses. Then, I am ready to go home for a bit of a clean-up, put on a fresh white dress and return to the hospital as doctor for my morning stint in the clinic or surgery or whatever is required of me, no longer matron or nurse, but doctor this time.

And so I take care of little girls who have poked big beans up their noses (the last one came off easily), see and talk to women who want babies and those who don't, try to discourage the fat women (Resht has a high quota of stylish stouts), from eating so much and encourage the thin ones to stop any senseless dieting and eat more, advise those who come to the prenatal clinic, treat the sick babies weekly in the Well Baby clinic, see some men and boys not reached by either Dr. Hoffman or our national assistant, Dr. Muradian, do minor or major surgery as needed, take almost all the baby cases as they come in night or day, and try to carry my share in this busy and crowded institution.

Of course, this is a mere outline of life, the chinks and cracks and open spaces are filled with the extras and that make life full and rounded and whole – the fellowship, the friendship, the joys and problems of living and working for Christ in this land of Islam.

Adelaide K. Hoffman

COLORS OF LIFE

Personal Report
June 1952

Remember 'way back when you used to look through a kaleidoscope, patterns of colored light and shadow? Let's look together at the past months of 1951-1952 as through a kaleidoscope and see what pattern of color, of events, of people come into view.

You cannot be long in this lush part of Iran without being aware of color, in the many shades of green in trees and grass, the delicate green of rice fields newly planted in the spring, the dark green of tea plants, the red tile roofs and red brick walls toned down by time and rain, the blue of the Caspian on a sunny day, and the bright profusion of flowers in our garden. And when driving out in the country you see the Persian woman's love of color expressed in the gay dress and *chaddor* she chooses to wear when in holiday mood or going to the bazaar. Even the fruits and vegetables being carried to market in reed baskets slung over the shoulder add their spots of bright colors. Last August, after we had closed the hospital, we flew from Teheran to Meshed for three happy weeks with friends there. During the three hours in the air we noticed especially the drab, grey-brown color of that part of Iran's mountains and plains until the city of Meshed came into view, when we glimpsed the golden dome of the Shrine and the glorious turquoise blue dome of the mosque shining in the brilliant mid-morning sun.

Turn the kaleidoscope once again. Following vacation come busy days getting Margie off to school in Teheran and the usual fall rush of patients is on in clinic and hospital, for the villagers come in after the rice is harvested to have old ailments mended and patched, not to mention the emergencies. In October, by turning just a little, you can see Rolla going off to Hamadan for a month to help out in the doctor shortage there caused by the Frames' sudden return to America[17]. You see me struggling along to reach to all duties put upon me by his absence and grateful for the help of my fellow missionaries and Dr. Muradian in the hospital. In early November bright, new figures emerge as the Dallas Landrums and little Stevie come from America to work in Resht, full of enthusiasm, and consecration and the desire to serve the Lord in Iran.

After a time these colors fade as in March the Landrums are refused residence permits in Resht, and Dallas must go to Teheran, later followed by Flora and Stevie, where they are still waiting for final word as to their status. December shows me in Teheran for an Executive Committee meeting, then Margie and I travel Reshtward through fields of white and past snowy mountain peaks. There is more gaiety and color in the home with Christmas and New Year's festivities. In February, by again turning our kaleidoscope, we see Rolla on an unexpected flight to America with a special patient, another emergency which he met during the year. I come into view surrounded by clamoring patients, carrying on for three weeks or more. But there is a gray color introduced here as we realize that our friend and colleague, Lynn Browning, long ill but every eager to keep on with his work for the Master, is

17   Dr. John Frame, Jr. and his family went out to Iran in 1947
            as missionaries and were assigned to the Hamadan Hospital.

finally beyond help. After the first week of March we no longer find him in our pictures. I must make two more trips to Teheran for meetings and to bring Margie home, along with a friend of hers for the summer vacation.

A kaleidoscope of color, of people, of events should also show guests coming in and out of the home – Adelaide going to church session meetings on alternate Friday afternoons, pumping the old church organ to squeeze out a little sound on Sunday mornings, seeing squalling, wiggly babies of a Wednesday clinic, getting up in the dark of the night for an obstetrical case, taking accounts with the hospital cook or dealing out sugar, or perhaps trying to help the young people of our pastor less church with the music of a play.

And so our simple kaleidoscope is really quite a remarkable instrument, for it has shown my life as it moved on through the days and the changing seasons of the past year. Now we are back to summer and a beautiful garden of color and light and shadow. But the best part is that such views through the kaleidoscope of our mind's eye reflect more than weaving colors and moving people and events. There is evident throughout all of our activities the guiding Hand of God, our loving Father as He leads us through shadow and sunlight.

Adelaide K. Hoffman

Photo 8.4 Resht Landscape – after rice harvest

CHANGING SCENES OF LIFE IN IRAN

Personal Report
June 1953

Time was years ago when I wrote with enthusiasm of the new and interesting things I saw or experienced. For instance I would have told about these: the bare-footed men I saw yesterday, digging a sewer ditch were taking time off for a 'coke', which for them was a small glass of tea, with accompanying lumps of sugar, borne to them on a brass tray; or the huge wooden trays piled high with strawberries, covered with green leaves for protection from sun and dust, carried into town daily this last month on the heads of sturdy men; or an old cart rattling down the street, the horse piloted by a work-blackened man, the load three large sacks of charcoal; or the twice daily fragrance of freshly cooked bread hanging in front of the bakery from a string on a peg, the long thin strips flapping in the wind; or the old clothes buyer as dilapidated as the wares he calls for as he wanders through the back streets; or even the few tired and bony carriage horses competing in their losing battle with the 50 or 60 taxis which the city now has. Perhaps I should write on the avenues – the sporty young man with a shirt of cloth printed to look like an illustrated newspaper (could that horror, undecipherable to him, be from the USA?), the movies with their huge billboards, the plastic utensils, the nylons, and so on.

What poverty, what riches in this land of the old and new! One often wonders how much is really desirable and worthwhile, how much is not so good. And what have I contributed this past year? Has it been worthwhile, my effort, and have I accomplished much? Here is my story for the year.

The year can be divided into a period before the first week in March and after that time, as far as my medical work goes. Since we had no national assistant doctor upon opening in September I gave almost my full time to the hospital, plus a few more minor jobs, which included our home, until March. This meant five morning clinics a week, with surgery sandwiched in on two mornings, also two afternoons, and one full day – the weekly prenatal clinic, Wednesday afternoon baby clinic, emergencies and hospital cook's accounts. This has been my life out here since in 1929 and I have become adjusted to it. I gladly gave some time to the church session until January, and have played the organ for all the church services. Then in

March our new Indian assistant doctor, Dr. Satralker, took my place in the hospital, to a certain extent, and I have felt a little more free for home and other duties, rather neglected at times.

There have been five trips to Teheran during the year, two for Executive Committee meetings and three to take Margaret either to or from Community school where she has finished the sixth grade. And now we are gathering up our possessions (oh, the folly and headache of so many possessions!) in preparation for our ten months furlough, which is very imminent. One of the very simple things I have recently begun, which I wish I had done months ago, is to help one of our promising young church boys with a love of music to learn some of the rudiments of playing the piano. He is a good pupil, and I hope with the aid of the Thompson books he will be able to continue by himself.

There in a few sentences are my labors for the year. One doesn't include all the little things that make life joyous, nor the times of discouragement that bring gray hairs and a sense of failure and frustration. And a missionary's life has a full measure of all these. But I keep on, for years ago my life was dedicated to the service of Jesus Christ, imperfect as that service may have turned out to be. The old is gradually superseded, whether it be in the changing, ongoing life around and within us, the advance in medical care and treatment or the growth of the spirit. For we do forget the things which are behind, 'and press on toward the goal unto the prize of the calling of God in Christ Jesus.'

Photo 8.5 Playing the organ for morning prayers at the hospital

The Eight-star Tile Plaque in Churches

Where once the wise men passed by caravan,

Thru desert plains to seek the Son of Man,

In His great Name we meet and lowly bow –

His ancient Star upon our pathway now;

And Persian hands have traced its rare design

In richly colored tile and flowing line.

One finds the dark blue center is His Name,

These eightfold attributes the circling frame.

The lowest one asserts His DEITY.

And clockwise, one may read the rest:

For he is called the SAVIOUR of mankind,

The HEALER, giving health and rest;

'Tis He DEFENDS the weakest and the poor,

And BUILDS and builds the temple of the Lord.

In His EXALTED NAME all men may find

FORGIVENESS promised thru the Word.

O, Star Divine, within our hearts abide,

Oh, Christ, be Thou our ever-present GUIDE.

Annonymous

CHAPTER 9

The Final Years 1954—1957

After a 10-month furlough we returned to Iran for the last few years of our life there. I returned to Community School again, living with different families each year. By this time it was a normal way of life, but Resht was always 'home'.

Before we left in the summer of 1953, the events leading up to the overthrow of Mossadegh and restoration of the Shah were becoming more intense. After hearing from family in the United States about how the situation was being reported, I remember thinking that the reporters were not distinguishing between the traditional religious parades in the evenings as part of *Moharram* and the political rallies and parades during the day. One day I was walking to the bazaar in Teheran when a large political parade and rally came down the middle of the main street. All of the shopkeepers came running out to the sidewalk and herded the pedestrians into the stores, dropped the grates down, closed the doors, and brought out the tea. While waiting for the rally to pass we drank tea and visited. Then the doors were opened and the grill raised while we thanked the shopkeeper and went on about our errands. In the following years we noticed more harassment towards us, even though we had lived in the same area for years.

BUSINESS AS USUAL

Personal Report
1954-1955

"Help me, no more children, *Khanum* doctor,"
"Help me, more children *Khanum*, doctor,"

was the perpetual refrain for this year's clinical work. 'Nothing succeeds like success' may sound trite, but apparently because of a few cases where the Lord and we have succeeded and new baby has made the mother and father happy, word has got around the countryside. As a result increasing numbers of patients come with the complaint 'For children' – both the sophisticated city women and the women of the villages. Yet in this country of contrasts the next complaint may be the opposite: 'I have enough children!' This seems to be the task, and the treatment thereof, Mondays through Saturdays. Sundays I forget babies and play the organ for church!

In between times I have done a few other things as missionary doctor, wife and mother. Our Margie, at 13 and a half, is full of energy, most of the time, and is always ready for a swim, a game of badminton or a book to read in her tree house. She is away at school in Teheran nine months of the year, and spends her Christmas and spring vacation here with us. Mother, or Daddy, or occasionally some other traveler, escorts her to Teheran or brings her home. And usually I make an extra trip during the year to see her.

Then there are the obstetrical cases, most of which I take care of with Miss Degner as my efficient substitute. And always I am grateful for the good help the nurses give in the long drawn out affairs. Monday afternoons I see from 15 to 20 or more tuberculosis patients for treatment and checkup. They are on the whole a much more cheerful and hopeful group than in the years past. Wednesday afternoon is Baby Clinic. From the crowds of mothers who come, this would seem like a refutation of half of my opening refrain, and a confirmation of the other. Child mortality is high, still very high. These hot summer days when candles melt to a 90-degree angle, are hard on the wee babies already weakened by semi-starvation and rickets, and in the winter its pneumonia and ear troubles in the inadequately clothed and cared for infants that carry them off. Thursday mornings has been the pre-natal clinic with surgery sandwiched in, and surgery also on Tuesday, Thursday and Saturday afternoon. Then there are also the daily hospital kitchen accounts to see to, nurses' classes for some weeks throughout the year, and of course taking over the hospital, with Dr. Satralker's (the Indian Christian assistant) help, whenever Dr. Hoffman is out of town.

This year we went through the discomfort of torn up living quarters, with dust and dirt and plaster and workmen everywhere, to emerge with a newly repaired and painted house, electric light wires newly buried, and new electric fixtures, all made clean and fresh. We are grateful for this lift to our home and our spirits, for here where we have little outside entertainment or recreation, and numbers of guests throughout the year coming and going, our homes are truly lived in.

Adelaide K. Hoffman

FAMILY LIFE

Resht, November 7, 1954

Dear Father and all,

A rainy Sunday afternoon is a good time to begin a letter to you. I am waiting for Rolla to return from Teheran – he is due most any minute now. He left for Teheran last Tuesday, was called in consultation on one of our crowd and likewise was glad of the chance for some errands there and to give his hands a 'rest'. Discouragingly, his allergic eruption flared up again – hands swelled up, blistered, and now are peeling all over again. It meant no operating for him so to get away for a few days was best for his morale. We don't seem to know exactly what is causing this dermatitis – the second attack since August. It is hard on us all. I think the few days in Teheran will have given him time to recover a bit, but the question still remains how to prevent another recurrence.

Yes, winter rains seem to have begun, though a lovely sunny day, or part of one, appears every so often. How fortunate it was that the iron roof on the hospital was finished before the more persistent rains began – only by a day or two! We were certainly grateful that it turned out so. Now they are busy on the inside construction and going ahead quite satisfactorily.

This week I have, perforce, been awfully busy in the hospital. So many come and are turned away even though we see as many as our strength and hours can take – often more than our brains can take. We have had plenty of surgery too – hope Rolla will be able to do some though I fear he won't for a time, as the surgical gloves and powder definitely seem to irritate his hands more and will have to be avoided. At least he will be here for consultation, which is a comfort.

Margie writes that she is coming home for Thanksgiving – something she has never been able to do before. It seems two of the young American women teachers in Community School, and two American soldier boys, are driving down here Wednesday afternoon at Gwen Belgum's invitation and have asked Margie to go along. They can stay until Sunday afternoon and then will drive back. I am not sure if they are coming in a jeep – perhaps – a rough ride on these roads, but I guess the young people can take it! Hope Iran gets down to business on her *roads* with all the American money being turned over to her that we hear about! Rolla will probably have more news of all the excitement about the Shah's brother's death – it happened after he left here. Any person who goes to Teheran always comes back with the news and 'gossip' both of country and mission for us all to hear.

We are planning to have the dinner at our house – probably on a community basis, inviting the other Americans – Point IV[18] – who are in town to come over, too. It will make a pretty big crowd if all come – some 25! We plan to use the nurse's classroom downstairs putting two tables in there, as our dining room is much too small

---

18　The **Point Four Program** was a technical assistance program for 'developing countries' announced by President Harry S. Truman in his inaugural address on January 20, 1949. Its name came from the fact that it was the fourth foreign policy objective mentioned in the speech. The idea was for a technical assistance program as a means to win the 'hearts and minds' of the developing world, by sharing US know-how in various fields, especially agriculture, industry and health.

for that many. Turkey we will have and the Point IVers have promised canned cranberry sauce. Guli (our cook) will buy the turkeys out in a village nearby.

Rolla hasn't turned up yet and I have an errand to do, so blessings on you and much love,

Adelaide

That trip in the back seat of the jeep was not one I want to repeat. Eight hours each way with no springs and just a sheepskin to sit on. I was frequently asked to accompany visitors as I spoke Farsi fluently and knew the area.

HOSPITAL NEEDS

Resht, January 10, 1955

Dear Harmon and Kaye,

The hospital building is progressing, but, my word, so many extras come up that we know not where all the money is coming from to pay for them. We have asked, through the mission of course, for permission from the Board to solicit funds up to $15,000 to help finish and equip the thing. It has already become quite a headache and we wonder how we are even going to live through the process of getting it ready for use! It would be fine if St. John's Church would like to give something – we will have a long list from which to choose. It does seem too bad with so much money being 'thrown around' by the American Government, as Point IV does here for instance, that we have to pinch so hard and struggle to get our small hospital even the minimum amount of necessary equipment. But then I guess that is the price paid for being independent of government, and working on faith that the Lord will provide. Perhaps we do not have enough of the latter.

Love to all of you from all of us,
Adelaide

JOYS OF TRAVEL

Resht, February 28, 1955

Dear Harmon,

My trip to Teheran started out in an annoying enough way – Saturday morning, the 19th, I got on the bus after saying goodbye, all set to go, started off and got as far as the Army Post outside the city where they check 'foreigners' and contraband. There the private on duty looked at my travel permit and announced it was three days overdue, whereas we thought it good for another month. He said I would have to get off the bus and get a new one – positively couldn't go! So down I came, couldn't argue too much as it was our mistake, though I was 'mad as a hatter'! Had the satisfaction of making them undo all the luggage and take off my suitcase! The Army post fixed me up in about five minutes when I went out – all het up and too late to get to Teheran that day. So I came home again and started off the next day without any 'red card', only the Army man's verbal order. It's a great life if you can take it! Coming back no one paid any attention to me. We think they push us around too much with all the U.S. is doing here.

The hospital is coming along fine – doors and windows going in, tiles being laid as the floors are done, plastering, and so on. It really looks like a building now and gives promise of being finished before too long. We are making plans for renovating the old building too – a lot of work needed there: the lower floor for the nurses, classes, rest, and dressing rooms, dining room, and so on; upper floor for private rooms, men and children. We've great ideas for making it look better and be more convenient – a new pantry and a dumb waiter which we've never had! There will be so much work necessary this summer we are not sure we can take a vacation – we shall see how it can be arranged.

We have been distressed these last few days by persecution, so to speak. One of our fine young Christian men – teaches in the school and well liked, but was told he would have to leave if he didn't give up Christianity – refused to do that and was given three days to reconsider. He still refused though his family is all against him. He thinks they will not put him out though he says he doesn't care now, he feels free and at peace, do what they will. It's hard for him especially with his family also being unsympathetic – to put it mildly.

> Our dear love to all of you,
> Adelaide

HOSPITAL IMPROVEMENTS

Christian Hospital
December 28, 1955

Dear Friends of St. John's Women Association,

Upon receiving the information of your gift of $1405, I at once acknowledged it in a note to Mrs. Hincks to thank her for her splendid efforts in raising the money, and you, the givers. I also said I would write you for what we had used it as soon as I could. The wheels of the Gods grind slowly. So far it has not yet been credited to the hospital's account though it has been received in the Teheran office. But now, as the year draws to a close, we are carefully going over the hospital's finances. (Don't worry I am not asking for more money!) We have decided that the $1405, from St. John's Women Association, will be used for the new electric autoclave (pressure sterilizer), which is the mainspring of any surgical unit. This has been ordered from Germany and will be soon arriving. Your gift will pay for most of it though we are not sure how much customs duty will be added on. This will be a most convenient and clean sterilizer to put into our beautiful new sterilizing room. Incidentally, our current one is now empty of any such for we could not bring our old one up there from the little outside room where it has been for years, as it is heated by a kerosene Primus stove. So you can imagine with what delight we will welcome this new one, and the nurses especially will bless you for it.

The new hospital is fine and a joy to work in, and we think with deepest gratitude of the many friends who have contributed to its convenience and efficiency.

Most sincerely yours,
Adelaide and Rolla

Photo 9.1 Resht Hospital after renovation and new addition

*Photo 9.2 Presenting diplomas
to graduate nurses*

*Photo 9.3 Capping ceremony for first year students with
Gwen Belgum*

Photo 9.4 Resht missionaries

CLINIC DAYS

Christian Hospital

Resht

Spring, 1956

Dear Friends,

In the springtime my garden is bursting into new life – the soft green of elm trees, white bridal wreath, purple and white iris, cala lilies, anemonies, and red roses, a lovely riot of bloom is beginning after the winter's dearth of flowers. With Easter just past the thought of new life springing up where death has been is still fresh in our minds, so I think of all the new little lives I have had a hand in bringing into this world this year, of the many babies, children and mothers I have had part in healing.

One often is tempted to wonder – where for many life is so very difficult, so impoverished, so lacking in the essentials like food, proper clothing and housing, not to mention the minor creature comforts we count so necessary – what life holds for them. But us Christian doctors don't dare to question that, just keep on trying to care for and serve the sick in the Name of Christ.

Here is little 'old' Gadali, 18 months of age when we started to treat him in the hospital, a wizened 'old man' with no teeth, unable to sit up or walk or talk, and weighing around five kilos, but breathing and living and still able to give a ghost of a smile. I saw him a few days ago in the Baby Clinic, sturdy little fellow now, weighing around nine kilos, 12 or more teeth, smiling and happy, almost babyish, and his family are very happy and proud. Two little newborn babies recently were brought in on the seventh or eighth day with the dread infection of tetanus, an unnecessary disease that takes a high toll of babies, infected at birth through the 'technique' of the midwife using a piece of dirty string or some superstitious practice. These two little ones we could not save. Another baby of two weeks I saw with a raw red lump on his tummy that proved to be an intestinal mass herniated through his navel and just left there since birth. He lived and was taken home well after surgery and antibiotics and nursing care.

Our Obstetrical department has been flourishing this winter since the new hospital opened up. We have always had such a high proportion of abnormal cases brought in to us, not only from villages and distant towns, but also our own city and neighbors, and we want them to feel they can rely on us. I have had to do a good many cesareans and the latest just went home, a woman of

30 who had lost two babies at birth and this third only had a chance if we did a Cesarean. She returned to her own town happy and proud of her little son. And there was the woman of around 95 kilos who had a Cesarean three years ago and this year was able to have her second child normally. One could go on and on with such tales, not all happy endings of course. And the picture is not complete without mentioning the women who are coming to the clinic in increasing numbers who have no children, or only one, and are desperate, for divorce or the threat of a second wife hangs over their heads. The raft of children in the streets makes one wonder how this can be so! Since I have had a few successes, more keep coming each clinic day.

This has been my job for 27 years. I have had to stick close to the hospital since this has been our policy, right or wrong. But one can see where the need is also in the villages far from a doctor – a poor mother was dragged 16 miles by horse to a small town, worked over there by several midwives and finally sent to us, having ridden many more miles by car over a terrible road in the cold, finally arriving at our door at 2 a.m., too far gone for help, though we tried. Perhaps we should have a new policy – more personnel, more equipment and move off to some of these isolated villages. My daughter Margie, now 14, having lived in a family of doctors and medical atmosphere is already talking of being a doctor and coming back to work in the villages of Iran.

Sincerely,
Adelaide K. Hoffman

Photo 9.5 Teenagers on summer vacation at the Caspian Sea

MODERN IRAN

Resht

October 31, 1956

Dear Friends,

With the reopening of the Resht Hospital September 1, after its annual August closing, we plunged into the final year of our allotted span in the Iran Mission.

In August we went for a final visit to Meshed, where we lived for so many years, 'long ago'. We rejoiced with them at the graduation of four nurses, we saw old friends, their children and grandchildren, we went to various picnics, teas and dinners, ending up with a moonlight picnic up on top of the nearby Stone Mountain. The hospital has been improved, and now has an attractive new entrance from the new, broad, paved avenue, which we had long anticipated in vain.

In September our school of nursing also had a graduation ceremony for a class of four nurses. Hospital work formally begins each morning with a brief assembly to seek God's guidance. The nurses, lab and office workers who attend this service over the years acquire a considerable knowledge of what Christianity stands for, even though many of them are not Christians. They like the atmosphere of a Christian hospital. A worker who spent some 15 years in the Meshed hospital called recently. He declared his years with us had been the happiest of his life.

"Folks asked me to become a Christian," he said, "but if I should do that, my neighbors would loot my store, and pelt my head with the very bricks from the floor."

Iran has taken her stand with the West by joining the Baghdad Pact. The Shah works constantly for reform. He has ordered a census taken, Iran's first; and he has said that he will, personally, teach a class of adults in the campaign against illiteracy. The Empress sponsors various charities and organizations for progress, including a medical congress held each year. A dramatic meeting of nursing educators, including advisors from Europe and America, was held recently in Teheran. Most of our Mission nurses attended, for they have done more than anyone else to build up schools of nursing. It is fine to have high standards, but we feel they have been set a bit too high, and may result in limiting the number of educated nurses to a comparatively few, who will be available only to the wealthy and a few larger hospitals. People now travel by bus, truck or bicycle-taxi, so of course they travel more, and bring home radios, and safety razors, with the result that beards are disappearing. And they wear city-made clothing. Schools are being built up, cooperatives organized by Point IV and roads are improved. Most women continue wearing the veil, though half-heartedly, and religious celebrations are more popular, with a sort of frenzied intensity.

The hospital's emphasis on the loving Christian care of the sick sets a standard we hope others will follow. The new and rapidly growing medical profession acquires medical knowledge more readily than high ethical standards, and lacks the motive of service.

Sincerely yours,
Adelaide and Rolla Hoffman

Photo 9.6 Staff Party

A REVIEW OF TWENTY-EIGHT YEARS

BEHIND THE VEIL

It is true that some 28 years ago, when I first began the practice of medicine in Iran, the women of this Moslem land were just beginning to take off the veil, not by their own initiative but by the vigorous efforts of the great reformer, Reza Shah Pahlavi, who aroused Iran from the sleep of ages. That was an extremely difficult phase for most women – heretofore they had believed that if any man other than father, brother or husband saw as much as one hair of their head they would be suspended by that hair over the fires of Hell. Now they were to appear unveiled in public, which naturally would include consulting a doctor in time of need. A woman might suffer and even die rather than allow herself to be exposed to a male physician, though a doctor legitimately could be considered an exception to this rule. The women of Iran are free now, they can go to a male doctor if they wish, and many do, but during my years in Iran I have found that on the whole many still prefer and appreciate the services of a female doctor. The old superstitions, outmoded ideas of their mothers and grandmothers are not cast aside easily, but like a moth struggling to free itself from the confinement of the cocoon it takes effort and will to accomplish it. Some have succeeded, others have not and maybe can, not partly because of the conservatism of their menfolk. They are 'behind the veil' and are calling for the help that only a woman doctor can give.

In the villages and small towns of Iran is where the women are bound down by the old taboos, and since a high percentage of the population is rural it is understandable that here the need is greatest. Our busy provincial mission hospitals are the focal point for crowds of villagers who come long distances on foot, horseback, by bus or car. I am called over to the hospital at 2 a.m. – a crowd of anxious appearing villagers in the upper hall surrounds a pallet on the floor where lies a woman, pale from hemorrhage and pain after several days of labor and mistreatment by numerous midwives. The baby is dead, the young mother is in bad condition, but there is hope for her. How grateful we all are when it is over and she is tucked into a clean bed to recuperate. Of course the call can come at any time of the day or night (on my first Christmas morning in Iran twins arrived, the last another future citizen), for a young mother who has not had proper or any prenatal care and is dragged in at the last moment.

A woman doctor expects to have busy nights, and days as well are filled with the seeing of sick folk and hearing their complaints. They come in droves, always with friends or relatives, from the wealthy city homes, from the middle class group such as teachers and clerks, from the poor, wretched hovels, and from the villages near and far. Often these folk are so picturesque in their long full skirts and gay overblouses – loaded with silver, even gold, and coins – and pretty young girls destined soon to look old with hard work and too frequent child bearing. The world over, it seems, women's diseases and pains are much the same. Here there are a few specialized troubles that stand out, most particularly the childless women, for in ignorance the woman is blamed and faces divorce or a second wife in the home. There can be no more grateful patient than one who can later report that now she has a little son or daughter. Then one's name and fame is spread abroad, though I always mention that it is the Lord's doing, not mine! Then there are those who come in from the villages with nutritional edema (swelling) of the extremities and profound anemia. One can help such a patient though it means constant reiteration of the necessity of proper food and vitamins, and not all the harmful dieting and fasting they have accepted for generations, handed down from mother to daughter.

The babies – wizened mites of skin and bone and big eyes – it is these little innocent ones that wring the heart. Never do I feel so depressed as after the free Baby Clinic when I see 25 to 35 sick babies week after week. Naturally the healthy and well-developed ones I do not see at this time. A frequent story behind a neglected sick baby is such desperate poverty that the mother is forced to leave the baby alone in the one room, or in the care of a six or seven-year-old, after fortifying it with an opium pill and a morning meal, while she spends the day working in the rice fields or tea gardens or silk factory, to support her husband's meager income. Small wonder this toothless, starved and doped, rachitic baby cannot sit up at 18 months. Yet even these pathetic little ones may manage a slight smile! We like to keep such a baby in our cheerful children's ward for a few weeks to watch the miraculous change come with good food, medicines and the prescription TLC – tender, loving, care – which every good nurse knows how to give. The infant mortality rate is high, no doubt less than 28 years ago, but it is still too much. Though the birth rate is up, the toll of babies dying under two years old is a heavy one. The Baby Clinic affords an opportunity to do a little pioneering in family planning and control – a needed service to those women who live behind the veil and are eager to better their lot and that of their children.

It is the older, more conservative women of Iran, and those who live in isolated communities who cling to the long established customs, while the younger city women welcome and readily adapt to their living the present amazing influx of modern gadgets and fashions. They would be shocked to think of themselves as behind the veil. Our hope and our prayer is that this great, immobilized force for good in the country – the women of Iran – may be aroused. There are signs of this on the horizon.

In 1957 Dr. Hoffman turned 70, the mandatory retirement age for missionaries. Even though my mother could have continued working in the hospital, and wanted to, the Mission Board insisted that she and Rolla leave the country and retire. Unfortunately, due to a shortage of mission doctors, hospitals had to gradually be closed, including our beloved hospital and home in Resht. Two years later the board asked my mother to return to Iran and keep the hospital open (as my parents had requested originally), but she felt she had been away from the practice of medicine too long to go back. By the mid-1960s most of the medical work in Iran no longer existed. The Resht Mission hospital was bought by an insurance company and operated with the Iranian staff and nurses who had been there before. The nurses, pharmacists and aides my mother had worked with, taught and trained, continued her work there.

The verses she had written in her diary in 1920 sustained her during these years of mission service, and on into retirement as she learned to live in the United States, now a foreign culture to her. What she had experienced in 1929 going out to Iran, she experienced in reverse coming back to California.

'Delight yourself in the Lord and He will give you
the desires of your heart.'

Psalm 37:4

'I can do all things through Christ who strengthens me.'

Philippians 4:13

Epilogue

The first few years of retirement and change of lifestyle are not easy for anyone. After being a busy doctor in another country, life in the United States was not easy to adjust to. Adelaide had her church work, and both Rolla and she became involved with the Foreign Student office at the University of California, hosting many students from the Middle East especially. Still, for 30 years of her life medicine had been her foremost activity. She considered renewing her medical license for California, but felt she had been away from the medical field in the United States too long. So much had changed over the years.

Rolla wrote his memoires of his life in Meshed, *Pioneering in Meshed, The Holy City of Iran; Saga of a Medical Missionary*. He also took up lawn bowling, in place of the tennis he had played in Iran. My mother, Adelaide, had never pursued any real hobby that she could do now, as medicine had always been the focus of her life. She mentioned in her letters how tedious it was for her to have to sew or do handicraft work.

In 1962 they moved from Oakland, to Monrovia, California, then in 1964 to Westminster Gardens, the Presbyterian retirement home in Duarte, California. Although she was much younger than most of the residents, there were fellow missionaries from Iran as well as from all over the world. Here they were both with people who had similar experiences in life and work. Adelaide was able to assist in the retirement home clinic, helping the doctor with women patients. This opportunity gave her much pleasure as she could again work in the medical field, although only in a limited capacity without a license. Rolla and she shared a sense of humor which the residents appreciated at gatherings, where he gave recitations and played musical numbers. He had a great collection of humorous stories and a sense of delivery that always made him popular and in demand for entertainment.

Traveling was one thing they both enjoyed, so over the years they took a number of cruises to various parts of the world they hadn't visited before, including a trip through the Panama Canal and countries in South East Asia.

Rolla died in 1974, and Adelaide continued to live at Westminster Gardens until her death in 1986. In the late 1970s, she developed macular degeneration of the eyes. It was a disease her mother had suffered and her sister, Laura, was also afflicted. From the time she got her driver's license at 16, driving had been one of her great pleasures. Now with the loss of her eyesight she had to give up driving friends and participating in the Meals on Wheels program. Laser treatment was able to slow the progress of the disease, but reading and driving were no longer possible.

I moved to Hawaii in 1963, married and had three children. Both Rolla and Adelaide enjoyed visiting us there, and my children became good travelers at an early age, going back and forth for visits to California.

Photo E1 Two grandmothers in Hawaii

Photo E2 Adelaide Kibbe Frame Hoffman - 1976

Adelaide died in 1986 after a stroke which left her paralyzed on one side, unable to eat or speak.

This is taken from her obituary: "Her work for the Monrovia Church and especially her concern for the continuance of missionary spirit in the group of 'Royal Daughters' were maintained by her quiet courage. And, when after the time of lingering in the known life, she slipped away from us into the new and glorious life, it was with the quietness that seemed appropriate to her calm courageous spirit."

The very path by which I wander

Shows glorious, golden, bathed in light;

No blade of grass that glistens yonder

But seems a star from heaven's height.

God's boundless love to His creation

Speaks through this beauty to my heart,

Fain would I, in rare exultation,

Sound through the world the wondrous message,

Of boundless love to all creation,

To all His love and joy impart.

Leo Tolstoy
(*Pilgrims' Song* by Tchaikovsky, lyrics by Tolstoy)

About the Author

Upon her parents' retirement, Margaret Frame completed high school in Oakland, California. After attending a local Community College, she moved to New York City and then to Hawaii where she graduated from the University of Hawaii with a degree in History. Marriage and family kept her in Hawaii for the next 17 years. A move to the mainland led her to Idaho for a further 17 years where she worked as a librarian and director of a small library.

In 1999, Margaret joined the Peace Corps and spent two years in Morocco working at the University of Kenitra. In order to continue working as a librarian she returned to graduate school and obtained an MLS (Masters in Library Science). Margaret worked as a librarian in Burlington County, New Jersey until her retirement in 2012. She currently lives in California.

Glossary

Abba – traditional long cloak worn by men

Agha – polite term used to address a man

Badji – house servant

Bazaaring – shopping

Caravanseri – historical rest areas used by travelers and caravans

Chilo – plain cooked rice

Chaddor – veil worn by women, material is sewn in large half circle and with straight edge held together over the face or under the chin

Droshky – horse drawn carriage, commonly seen today for rides in parks

Faresch – measurement of distance, one *faresch* = 14 miles

Galamcars – fabric printed using wooden stamps

Gilan – province in northern Iran

Hamal – person for hire who hauls goods, usually on their back

Hose – pool in the yard used as water source

Insha'allah – God willing

Jube – deep, open, water ditch alongside of roads

Kafir – Islamic term for infidel or unbeliever

Khanum – polite term used to address a woman

Khaki – tan dirt, which in English is the color khaki

Koresh – stew of vegetables or fruit with meat served over plain rice

Kran – small denomination coin

Kucheh – small alleys

Kursi – a low table with pan of charcoal underneath and covered with quilts surrounded by pillows and more quilts, around which the family sits for warmth during the winter

Kuseh – clay water jug

Mash'allah – Allah's blessing

Mirza – title of respect for a learned man, for example used to denote someone with medical training

Moharram – Shiite month of mourning in remembrance of the death of Hassan and Hosein

Mullah (Mollah) – learned Moslem holy man, leader of Friday prayers at Mosques

Pilow (pilo) – rice cooked with vegetables or fruit and meat

Pustein – embroidered sheepskin coats

Ramadan – Moslem month of fasting

Rosh khan – prayer meeting during the month of *Moharram*

Savab – spiritual reward or merit

Sharbat – a sweet fruit drink

Takhcheh – shelf built into wall

Tomans – monetary unit

NOTE ON PRONUNCIATION:

The transliteration of Farsi words into English is based on traditional Farsi pronunciation. In Farsi the last syllable is accented, for example – *chad-DORE*. Exceptions are loan words from Arabic in which the first or middle syllable is emphasized – *MASH'allah* and *INSHA'allah*. The names of cities are spelled as pronounced in the local area. For example, many maps spell the city of Resht as 'Rasht', which is not the correct pronunciation in Gilan.

Suggested Reading

Abrahamian, Ervand. *Iran Between Two Revolutions. Princeton*, N.J.: Princeton University Press, 1982.

Abrahmian, Ervand, *A History of Modern Iran*. New York: Cambridge University Press, 2008.

Al-Saltana, Taj. *Crowning Anguish: Memoirs of a Persian Princess from the Harem to Modernity*. Washington, D.C.: Mage, 2003.

Ansari, Ali M. *Modern Iran Since 1921: The Pahlavis and After*. London: Pearson, 2003.

Banani, Amin. *The Modernization of Iran, 1921-1941*. Stanford, Calif.: Stanford University Press, 1961.

Bellaigue, Christopher de. *Patriot of Persia: Mohammad Mossadegh and a Tragic Anglo-American Coup*. New York: HarperCollins, 2012.

Bill, James A. *The Eagle and the Lion: The Tragedy of American-Iranian Relations*. New Haven, Conn.: Yale University Press, 1988.

Cronin, Stephanie, ed. *The Making of Modern Iran: State and Society Under Riza Shah 1921-1941*. London: RoutledgeCurzon, 2003.

Dabashi, Hamid. Iran: *A People Interrupted*. New York: New Press, 2007.

Elm, Mostafa. *Oil, Power, and Principle: Iran's Oil Nationalization and Its Aftermath*. Syarcuse, N.Y.: Syracuse University Press, 1992.

Farman Farmaian, Sattareh, and Dona Munker. *Daughter of Persia: A Woman's Journey from Her Father's Harem Through the Islamic Revolution*. New York: Crown, 1992.

Forbis, William H. *Fall of the Peacock Throne: The Story of Iran*. New York: McGraw-Hill, 1981.

Ghani, Cyrus. *Iran and the Rise of Reza Shah: From Qajar Collapse to Pahlavi Power*. London: I.B. Tauris, 1998.

Keddie, Nikki R. *Modern Iran: Roots and Results of Revolution*. New Haven, Conn.: Yale University Press, Updated 2006.

Kinzer, Stephen. *All the Shah's Men: An American Coup and the roots of Middle East Terror*. New York: Wiley, 2003.

Mackey, Sandra. *The Iranians: Persia, Islam, and the Soul of a Nation*. New York: Dutton, 1996.

Polk, William R. *Understanding Iran: Everything You Need to Know, from Persia to the Islamic Republic, from Cyrus to Ahmadinejad*. New York: Palgrave MacMillan, 2009.

Sciolino, Elaine. *Persian Mirrors: The Elusive Face of Iran*. New York: Free Press, 2000.

Wilber, Donald. *Riza Shah Pahlavi: The Resurrection and Reconstruction of Iran, 1878-1944*. Hicksville, N.Y.: Exposition Press, 1975.

Also Published by Summertime Publishing

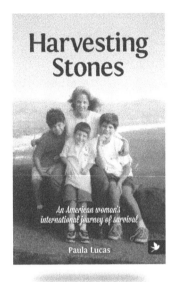

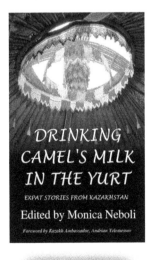

FLY AWAY
HOME

Maggie Myklebust

SUNSHINE
SOUP

NOURISHING THE GLOBAL SOUL

Jo Parfitt

WHAT ABOUT YOUR SAUCEPANS?

LINDSAY DE FELIZ

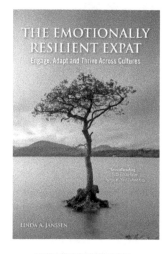

THE EMOTIONALLY
RESILIENT EXPAT

Engage, Adapt and Thrive Across Cultures

LINDA A. JANSSEN

Milton Keynes UK
Ingram Content Group UK Ltd.
UKHW011701020424
440487UK00002B/454

9 781909 193574